Palgrave Studies in Cybercrime and Cybersecurity

Series Editors
Thomas J. Holt, Michigan State University, East Lansing, USA
Cassandra Cross, School of Justice, Queensland University of
Technology, Brisbane, Australia

This book series addresses the urgent need to advance knowledge in the fields of cybercrime and cybersecurity. Because the exponential expansion of computer technologies and use of the Internet have greatly increased the access by criminals to people, institutions, and businesses around the globe, the series will be international in scope. It provides a home for cutting-edge long-form research. Further, the series seeks to spur conversation about how traditional criminological theories apply to the online environment. The series welcomes contributions from early career researchers as well as established scholars on a range of topics in the cybercrime and cybersecurity fields. Original series creators and co-founders: Marie-Helen Maras and Thomas J. Holt.

Asher Flynn · Elena Cama · Adrian J. Scott

Image-Based Sexual Abuse and Bystander Intervention

A Mixed Methods Study of Attitudes, Barriers and Facilitators

Asher Flynn (ID)
Monash University, Australian
Research Council Centre
of Excellence for the Elimination
of Violence Against Women
Clayton, VIC, Australia

Elena Cama (ID)
Centre for Social Research in Health
UNSW Sydney
Kensington, NSW, Australia

Adrian J. Scott (ID)
Department of Psychology
Goldsmiths, University of London
London, UK

ISSN 2946-2770   ISSN 2946-2789   (electronic)
Palgrave Studies in Cybercrime and Cybersecurity
ISBN 978-3-031-83646-6   ISBN 978-3-031-83647-3   (eBook)
https://doi.org/10.1007/978-3-031-83647-3

This Palgrave Macmillan imprint is published by the registered company Springer Nature Switzerland AG
The registered company address is: Gewerbestrasse 11, 6330 Cham, Switzerland

If disposing of this product, please recycle the paper.

Acknowledgements We would like to thank the many individuals that helped shape and contribute to this project. In particular, we express our gratitude to the 245 participants, who gave up their valuable time to contribute their perspectives on this significant and growing social and legal issue.

We also wish to acknowledge the funding and support received from the Australian Criminology Research Council to undertake the study (CRG02/18-19). We hope that this research will contribute to more effective ways of responding to, and preventing, the occurrence of image-based sexual abuse, and improve bystander awareness of potential interventions that can be safely used to help support victim-survivors and disrupt abusive behaviours.

Finally, we would like to thank our friends, family, and colleagues for their continued support.

Ethics Approval This project received ethics approval from the Monash University Human Research Ethics Committee (Project No. 17905). All participants were provided with an explanatory statement and signed a consent form prior to engaging in the research.

CONTENTS

ABOUT THE AUTHORS

Dr. Asher Flynn is a Professor of Criminology at Monash University and a Chief Investigator on the Australian Research Council Centre of Excellence for the Elimination of Violence Against Women (CEVAW), where she leads the technology-facilitated violence workstream and is Deputy Lead of Research Ethics & Training. Asher is an award-winning researcher in policy and prevention concerning gendered, sexual, and technology-facilitated violence. She has published eight books and over 120 articles, scholarly book chapters, reports, and media/opinion pieces. Her research has informed international laws on image-based sexual abuse and sexual violence. She is the recipient of prestigious national and international research fellowships and is Editor-in-Chief of the *Journal of Criminology*. Asher has advised the Australian Office of the eSafety Commissioner, the United Nations, Meta, and Bumble on policy and prevention concerning technology-facilitated gender-based violence.

Dr. Elena Cama is a Postdoctoral Researcher at the Centre for Social Research in Health at the University of New South Wales, Sydney. She is a mixed methods researcher with a background in criminology, social science, and public health. Her research has focused on experiences, impacts, and responses to marginalisation, discrimination, and violence. This work has included a focus on sexual harms experienced in a range of contexts, including those facilitated via dating and hook-up apps, in the context of using taxi and rideshare services, in the night-time economy, and in higher education settings.

Dr. Adrian J. Scott is a Reader of Psychology (Associate Professor) at Goldsmiths, University of London, where he is Co-Director of the Forensic Psychology Unit and of an accredited M.Sc. program in Forensic Psychology. Adrian is a chartered psychologist with associate fellow status within the British Psychological Society and has a broad interest in forensic psychology, specialising in the areas of stalking, image-based sexual abuse, investigative interviewing, and eyewitness testimony.

LIST OF TABLES

CHAPTER 1

Introduction

Abstract Image-based sexual abuse—the non-consensual creation, taking, sharing, or threat to share nude or sexual images—is a growing global issue, with research demonstrating that this form of technology-facilitated sexual violence is common and increasing. Image-based sexual abuse continues to occur partly because individuals actively or passively support inequality, discriminatory attitudes, or violence; remain silent; and/or tolerate the abuse and its underlying causes. Intervention by people who witness image-based sexual abuse behaviours, referred to as bystander intervention, has the potential to reduce the extent and impact of image-based sexual abuse, problematic attitudes, and harms. In this regard, bystanders are an untapped resource and have a potentially greater role to play in the prevention of image-based sexual abuse. In this chapter, we summarise the key definitions and literature relevant to image-based sexual abuse. We also conceptualise bystander intervention and provide an overview of the effectiveness of bystander intervention programs in the context of sexual violence. This chapter concludes with an outline of the book.

Keywords Image-based sexual abuse · Bystander · Intervention · Sexual violence

A. Flynn et al., *Image-Based Sexual Abuse and Bystander Intervention*, Palgrave Studies in Cybercrime and Cybersecurity, https://doi.org/10.1007/978-3-031-83647-3_1

1

INTRODUCTION

In January 2024, non-consensually created sexually explicit fake imagery of Taylor Swift was distributed on several social media platforms (Flynn et al., 2024b). The images were examples of a rapidly emerging form of image-based sexual abuse, known as sexualised deepfake abuse (or 'deepfakes'), in which artificial intelligence technologies are used to create realistic, but partially or entirely fabricated non-consensual sexualised images, recordings, or videos of another person (Flynn et al., 2022a). Image-based sexual abuse—whether involving real or deepfake imagery—is a form of technology-facilitated sexual violence that involves the non-consensual creation, taking, distribution, and/or threat to distribute nude or sexual imagery of another person. Over the past ten years, there has been substantial scholarly and public attention paid to image-based sexual abuse globally (Flynn et al., 2022a, 2022b, 2023a; Henry et al., 2020; McGlynn et al., 2021), with research finding that perpetration and victimisation is relatively common (Blais et al., 2024; Eaton et al., 2018; Henry et al., 2020; Lenhart et al., 2016; Patel & Roesch, 2022; Powell et al., 2019a, 2019b; Snaychuk & O'Neill, 2020) and increasing (Powell et al., 2022a, 2022b). Consistent among these studies is a higher rate of victimisation among people who are gender and sexuality diverse, from ethnic or racial minorities, Indigenous and First Nations people, and from younger cohorts, mirroring other forms of sexual violence (Eaton et al., 2018; Flynn et al., 2022a, 2024c; Henry et al., 2020; Lenhart et al., 2016; Patel & Roesch, 2022; Powell et al., 2022a, 2022b). Research has also found that image-based sexual abuse can cause significant social, physical, psychological, and economic harms (Bates, 2017; Flynn & Henry, 2021; McGlynn et al., 2021; Powell et al., 2018).

Many countries have criminalised the non-consensual distribution of nude or sexual images (Flynn, 2023), and increasingly, jurisdictions are criminalising threats to distribute such images, as well as the non-consensual creation, sharing, or threat to share sexualised deepfake imagery (Flynn et al., 2022a, 2022b, 2024b). However, while the introduction of specific laws is a positive step towards recognising the harms and experiences of victim-survivors, there continue to be several barriers to reporting and prosecuting image-based sexual abuse, and to shifting problematic attitudes around victim-blaming and minimising the harms of this form of sexual violence (Bothamley & Tully, 2018; Flynn et al., 2023a, 2023b; Henry et al., 2018).

One of the reasons that image-based sexual abuse continues to occur is because individuals actively or passively support inequality, discriminatory attitudes, or violence; remain silent; and/or tolerate the abuse and its underlying causes (Flynn et al., 2024a; VicHealth, 2011). Indeed, research suggests that intervention by people who witness abusive behaviours can reduce the extent and impacts of these behaviours, problematic attitudes, and harms (Barlińska et al., 2013; Brochado et al., 2017; Kowalski et al., 2014; Rebollo-Catalan & Mayor-Buzon, 2020; Song & Oh, 2018). Bystander action or intervention refers to words and actions that are taken by those not directly involved in a critical event, to disrupt, prevent, or respond to that event. The concept emerged from social psychology and was a key focus of study following World War II when researchers sought to examine why people remained passive or did not intervene to prevent the Holocaust (Powell, 2011). Researchers have since been interested in how bystanders respond in emergency situations, how their behaviours are influenced by the actions of other bystanders, the barriers and facilitators to intervention, and programs that can help encourage bystanders to safely intervene. Specifically, research has found that promoting bystanders to speak up or take action when they witness violence or discrimination may be an effective prevention tool (Darley & Latané, 1968; Dovidio et al., 2006; Gordon-Messer et al., 2013; Latané & Darley, 1970). In this regard, bystanders are an untapped resource and have a potentially greater role to play in the prevention of image-based sexual abuse.

Returning here to Taylor Swift's victimisation experience, the social media platforms on which the content was shared were very slow to respond. Instead, it took millions of bystanders joining what was referred to as a 'mega-reporting campaign' (NBC, 2024)—in which individual users reported any accounts that were sharing the images—before offending accounts were suspended and the images removed, some 19 hours and 45 million views later (Goujard, 2024). Individuals also engaged in bystander action which made it harder to find the images by flooding the trending hashtags (e.g. #TaylorSwiftAI) with positive messages about Taylor Swift and creating new trending hashtags (e.g. #ProtectTaylorSwift), so when people searched for the images or searched for 'Taylor Swift', they found different threads and trending stories. Bystander intervention was also taken by placing pressure on social media and digital platforms to remove the imagery, with users posting messages condemning the actions of those creating or sharing the images without consent, contributing to a public discourse around how such behaviour breaches social norms and standards.

While this situation provides evidence of innovative and collective bystander intervention, as one of the world's biggest celebrities, Taylor Swift is in quite a unique situation. As Goldberg observed at the time, 'most human beings don't have millions of fans who will go to bat for them if they've been victimised' (cited in Woods, 2024). This is not simply because people do not care, or that bystanders are not witnessing image-based sexual abuse, but rather because many people do not have the knowledge, skills, or confidence to safely intervene (Flynn et al., 2024a). This highlights the importance of building the evidence-base on silent and passive bystanders versus 'prosocial' or 'active' bystanders (Darley & Latané, 1968; Latané & Darley, 1970; see also Clarke, 2003; Dovidio et al., 2006) to better understand bystander intervention in the context of image-based sexual abuse. This book responds to this challenge.

In this book, we present analyses from the first mixed methods study to focus specifically on bystander intervention in image-based sexual abuse contexts. The study sought to examine attitudes towards, and awareness of, image-based sexual abuse, applicable laws, and available options/ remedies to respond to, or counter, such behaviours. Specifically, we focused on people's willingness or preparedness to intervene, and the barriers and facilitators to bystander action. Ultimately, the two primary aims of the study were to:

1. Understand bystander attitudes towards image-based sexual abuse, and measure their capacity and willingness to intervene when witnessing these behaviours, and
2. Identify the key influencing factors for bystanders, including the barriers and facilitators to intervention, when they witness image-based sexual abuse.

To address these aims, we conducted an online, anonymous survey with 245 Australian residents (aged 18–71 years) and 35 in-person focus groups with 219 participants across Australia.

In this chapter, we present a review of the existing literature on bystander intervention programs and their effectiveness. We begin by defining image-based sexual abuse and presenting a brief background on its prevalence, nature, and impacts. We then conceptualise bystanders and bystander intervention, and discuss evidence on the efficacy of bystander intervention programs in the context of sexual violence. We conclude with an overview of the book chapters that will follow.

A Brief Note on Terminology

We use the term 'image-based sexual abuse' throughout the book to refer to the non-consensual creation, taking, distribution, or threat to distribute nude or sexual imagery, including static photographic images (such as screenshots or photographs) and videos. Image-based sexual abuse can also be referred to as 'image-based abuse' (Flynn & Henry, 2021), 'non-consensual intimate imagery' (Flynn et al., 2024a), 'non-consensual pornography' (Franks, 2017), and perhaps most problematically, 'revenge pornography' (Bond & Tyrell, 2021; see Henry et al., 2020 for a discussion on the issues with using this term). As we explain in Chapter 2, during the survey and focus groups, we used the term 'non-consensual imagery' rather than image-based sexual abuse to reduce the potential for the terminology to influence participants' perceptions. However, we report on these data using the term image-based sexual abuse for consistency and clarity in the book.

Throughout the book, we use the term 'perpetrator' to refer to someone who has engaged in any image-based sexual abuse behaviours and 'victim-survivor' to refer to someone who has experienced any image-based sexual abuse behaviours. We recognise that there are divergent opinions around the appropriate terminology to accurately represent perpetration and victimisation experiences, and that many people who have experienced image-based sexual abuse may not identify with the terms victim or survivor. However, for the purpose of this book and with the utmost consideration of those who have experienced image-based sexual abuse, we use this terminology to represent the potential harms of these behaviours, and to recognise that responsibility for these behaviours rests solely with the perpetrator, not the victim-survivor. Finally, when reporting on the focus group data, we use the term S1 and S2 to refer to hypothetical Scenario 1 and hypothetical Scenario 2, respectively (see Table 2.8 in Chapter 2 or Appendix Table A.1 for details of the scenarios).

Prevalence and Harms
of Image-Based Sexual Abuse

Digital technologies have facilitated many beneficial social and cultural changes globally, but they are also implicated in the perpetration of harmful, abusive, and illegal behaviours (Bailey et al., 2021; Cama, 2021; Flynn et al., 2024c; Henry et al., 2020; Powell & Flynn, 2023). The dominant role of digital technologies in people's lives and the instantaneous and widespread sharing power of the internet have created an environment where harms such as image-based sexual abuse, sexual harassment, and domestic and family violence are not only possible, but can be facilitated in new and powerful ways (Flynn et al., 2024c; Henry et al., 2020). Taylor Swift's recent victimisation represents one such new form of sexual violence (Flynn et al., 2024b).

Research suggests that experiences of sexual violence facilitated by, or perpetrated through, digital technologies are common. The most comprehensive survey of online harassing behaviour in the United States to date was undertaken by the Pew Research Center (2021). In its representative survey of over 10,000 adults, 41% reported having been personally subjected to harassing behaviour online (Pew Research Centre, 2021). Women, and young women in particular, were significantly more likely than men to experience sexualised forms of abuse, with 16% of all women and 33% of women under 35 years reporting having been sexually harassed online, compared with 5% of all men and 11% of men under 35 years (Pew Research Center, 2021). In the Australian context, a nationally representative survey of over 4,500 Australian adults found that 51% reported experiencing technology-facilitated violence in their lifetime (Powell et al., 2022a, 2022b, 2022c). Most commonly, participants reported that they had experienced monitoring and controlling behaviours (33.7%), followed by emotional abuse and threats (30.6%), harassing behaviours (26.7%), and sexual and image-based abuse (24.6%) (Flynn et al., 2024c). Although men and women reported similar rates of overall victimisation, women reported experiencing greater harms because of their experiences, including fearing for their safety (26% women; 13% men), and experiencing repeated abuse from the same person (28% women; 19% men) (Powell & Flynn, 2023). Women were also more likely to report experiencing the abuse from a current or former partner (40% women; 32% men), and to report that the person tried to control them in other ways beyond the online abuse (33% women; 25% men) (Powell & Flynn, 2023).

The available empirical research on image-based sexual abuse similarly suggests that experiences of these behaviours are relatively common. However, variations in terminology and measurement make it challenging to estimate prevalence of both victimisation and perpetration across studies (Paradiso et al., 2024; Walker & Sleath, 2017). Patel and Roesch (2022) conducted a systematic review and meta-analysis to determine the prevalence of technology-facilitated sexual violence, including image-based sexual abuse. Findings from 19 articles comprising 32,247 participants revealed pooled prevalence victimisation rates of 17.6% having had their intimate image taken without consent, 8.8% having had their intimate image shared without consent, and 7.2% having been threatened with the distribution of their intimate image. A study by Henry et al. (2019a) of more than 4,000 Australians aged 16 to 49 years found that as many as one in five reported having experienced at least one form of image-based sexual abuse (taking, sharing, threat to share). The majority of the perpetrators in Henry et al.'s (2019a) study were reported to be men and known to the victim-survivor, such as a current or former intimate partner.

The most comprehensive research on the prevalence, nature, and impacts of image-based sexual abuse to date has been conducted by Henry et al. (2020) and Powell et al. (2022a, 2022b). In their survey of participants aged 16 to 64 years across Australia ($n = 2,054$), New Zealand ($n = 2,027$), and the United Kingdom ($n = 2,028$), Powell et al. (2022a) reported that 38% of participants had experienced at least one form of image-based sexual abuse victimisation, with the figures being comparable across the three countries (Australia, 35%; New Zealand, 39%; United Kingdom, 39%). Of those surveyed, 47% of those aged 16 to 39 years had experienced one or more forms of image-based sexual abuse, compared with 26% of participants aged 40 to 64 years. Further research from this study, specifically examining sexualised deepfake abuse, found that 14.1% of participants had experienced one or more forms of sexualised deepfake abuse, including 11.3% experiencing its creation, 10.4% distribution, and 10.1% the threat to distribute (Flynn et al., 2022a). In another study reporting on data from over 16,000 participants across 10 countries, researchers found that 2.2% reported having experienced some form of sexualised deepfake abuse, which included the creation, distribution, or threat to distribute imagery (Umbach et al., 2024).

Research on prevalence has further shown that image-based sexual abuse disproportionately impacts gender and sexuality diverse people, people living with a disability, and Indigenous and First Nations people (Eaton et al., 2018; Henry et al., 2019a, 2019b; Office of the eSafety Commissioner, 2017). For example, Powell et al. (2022a) found that 56% of gender and sexuality diverse participants compared with 35% of heterosexual participants, and 66% of Indigenous and First Nations participants compared with 34% of non-Indigenous and First Nations participants, reported having experienced one or more forms of image-based sexual abuse.

More recently, researchers have turned to understanding the perpetration of image-based sexual abuse. A recent scoping review into perpetration of image-based sexual abuse found that most research has focused on the non-consensual distribution of intimate images, with less attention paid to other forms of image-based sexual abuse, such as the non-consensual taking or creation of intimate images and sexualised deepfake abuse (Henry & Beard, 2024). In their systematic review and meta-analysis, Patel and Roesch (2022) reported pooled perpetration prevalence rates of 8.9% having taken an intimate image without consent, 12% having shared an intimate image without consent, and 2.7% having threatened to share intimate images without consent. Research among 3,044 adults in the United States found that one in 20 reported ever having shared an intimate image without that person's consent (Ruvalcaba & Eaton, 2020). Similar findings arose from a survey of 1,200 Canadian adults, with 5.1% reporting ever having disseminated non-consensual intimate images (Blais et al., 2024).

Across Australia, New Zealand, and the United Kingdom, researchers found that 15.8% of over 6,100 people admitted to having ever taken intimate images without consent, 10.6% admitted to sharing intimate images without consent, and 8.8% reported threatening to share intimate images without consent (Powell et al., 2022b). Further research from this study found that 7.5% of participants had engaged in one or more forms of sexualised deepfake abuse, including 5.4% creation, 4.4% distribution, and 4.2% threaten to distribute (Flynn et al., 2022a). Finally, in surveys comprising 16,000 people across 10 countries, 1.8% reported some form of perpetration of sexualised deepfake abuse involving either creation, distribution, or threat to distribute (Umbach et al., 2024).

Research has found that perpetrators of image-based sexual abuse can be intimate partners, family members, friends, acquaintances, and persons unknown to the victim-survivor (Powell et al., 2019a, 2019b). Image-based sexual abuse occurs in a range of contexts, including relationship break-ups, sextortion, voyeurism (e.g. 'upskirting' and 'downblousing'), sexploitation, and sexual assault (Powell et al., 2019a, 2019b). There is limited knowledge around demographic risk factors for perpetration, with some evidence to suggest that men and younger adults are more likely to self-report the perpetration of image-based sexual abuse behaviours (Blais et al., 2024; Henry & Beard, 2024; Paradiso et al., 2024). There is further evidence that those who are more likely to accept myths around image-based sexual abuse that minimise the harms or excuse the perpetrator are also more likely to perpetrate image-based sexual abuse (Paradiso et al., 2024).

Image-based sexual abuse is widely recognised as a significant public health problem owing to the multiple psychological, physical, social, and economic harms individuals experience because of image-based sexual abuse, including anxiety, depression, suicidal ideation, social isolation, and financial loss (Bates, 2017; Citron & Franks, 2014; Cyber Civil Rights Initiative, 2014; Henry et al., 2020). Henry et al. (2020) found that victim-survivors experience distress, negative health impacts, reputational concerns, and negative impacts on their relationships with others. Some researchers have found the impacts of image-based sexual abuse to be gendered, with women more likely to experience distress, negative health impacts, reputational concerns, and relational impacts compared to men (Eaton et al., 2018; Henry et al., 2020; Powell et al., 2022a). However, others critique image-based sexual abuse as a gendered harm, with some evidence to suggest that men experience similar sentiments as women, such as feelings of loss of control and fears around future experiences of victimisation (Champion et al., 2022). McGlynn and colleagues (2021) report that the impacts of image-based sexual abuse are pervasive and include 'social rupture', which refers to an all-encompassing devastation or disruption to one's everyday life, relationships, and activities.

RESPONDING TO IMAGE-BASED SEXUAL ABUSE

Over the past ten years, there has been greater attention paid to image-based sexual abuse globally, evidenced by parliamentary inquiries, public consultations, criminal law reform, media attention, as well as other proposed or enacted legal and non-legal measures (see, e.g., Flynn, 2023; Henry et al., 2019a, 2020; Kirchengast, 2020). All but one of Australia's

eight state and territory jurisdictions (Tasmania excluded) have introduced specific offences to criminalise image-based sexual abuse, with most
including laws that capture the non-consensual distribution of sexualised
deepfake imagery. The Australian Commonwealth Government introduced laws in August 2018 to specifically criminalise image-based sexual
abuse at a federal level (Flynn & Henry, 2021), resulting in some prosecutions across Australia (see Henry et al., 2020). Most recently, this
included a man who was imprisoned in New South Wales for uploading
hundreds of sexualised deepfake images of 26 women to pornographic
websites, alongside graphic descriptions of rape and violent assault (ABC,
2024). Federal legislation was amended in 2024 to better capture sexualised deepfake abuse as a form of image-based sexual abuse (*Criminal
Code Act 1995* (Cth); *Criminal Code Amendment (Deepfake Sexual Material Bill 2024* (Cth)). While the introduction of specific image-based
sexual abuse laws in Australian jurisdictions is a positive step towards
recognising its harms and the experiences of victim-survivors, research
to date has found that there is limited understanding among Australians
of the existence and scope of these laws, how and when they apply,
and who to approach for help (Flynn, 2023; Flynn & Henry, 2021;
Henry et al., 2019a, 2020; Office of the eSafety Commissioner, 2017).
There also continue to be several barriers to reporting image-based sexual
abuse, including a lack of police resources, evidentiary issues, jurisdic-
tional restrictions, and victim-blaming attitudes among police and society
that minimise and trivialise image-based sexual abuse (Flynn et al., 2023a;
Henry et al., 2018; McGlynn et al., 2021).

The low reporting of image-based sexual abuse to the police, and
subsequent low numbers of image-based sexual abuse prosecutions
(Henry et al., 2018, 2019a), has created a sizeable gap between estimated image-based sexual abuse victimisation and official reporting and
prosecution rates of perpetration. For example, 35% of Australian participants in one study reported having experienced image-based sexual abuse
(Henry et al., 2020), yet research conducted by the Office of the eSafety
Commissioner (2017) estimated that only one in four Australians who
experience image-based sexual abuse take action, such as reporting the
abuse. Data from police reports further demonstrate the gap between
image-based sexual abuse victimisation, official reporting rates, and criminal justice outcomes. A report released by the Victorian Sentencing
Advisory Council (Chalton & Schollum, 2020), for example, showed that
2,055 image-based sexual abuse offences were recorded by the police

in the four-year study period (2015–2016 to 2018–2019). Of these, only 23% were sentenced, with outcomes including community correction orders, imprisonment, and fines.

Further to low reporting and prosecution rates, there are relatively low numbers of bystander intervention in image-based sexual abuse incidents, as well as online harassment more broadly, recorded in research. In the next sections, we explore some of the research on bystanders and bystander intervention generally, before specifically exploring the research on bystander intervention and image-based sexual abuse.

BYSTANDERS AND BYSTANDER INTERVENTION

A bystander refers to a person who witnesses or is aware of an emergency or critical event, such as harmful behaviour or a harmful event that is happening to another person (Taket & Crisp, 2017). Bystander action or intervention refers to words and actions that are taken by those not directly involved in the critical event to disrupt or prevent the event from occurring. One prominent theory on bystanders relates to the bystander effect. Darley and Latané (1968) are credited with first conceptualising and examining the concept of the bystander effect, which refers to the phenomenon whereby a person's likelihood of intervening when witnessing a critical event decreases in the presence of other bystanders who do not intervene. Darley and Latané (1968) suggested that if an individual is alone and notices an emergency situation, they will feel a greater sense of responsibility to intervene than if there are other people present who could intervene in their place. These authors theorised that there were three elements fuelling the bystander effect: (1) the diffusion of responsibility, whereby the greater the number of bystanders present, the less personal responsibility the bystander will feel to intervene; (2) evaluation apprehension or fears of being judged or viewed negatively as a result of intervention (e.g. being perceived as intervening when they should not or intervening in an inappropriate way); and (3) social influence, or how other bystanders react in situations. Although there is evidence to suggest that the presence of passive bystanders in critical situations reduces the helping responses of bystanders, a meta-analysis by Fischer and colleagues (2011) found that such a reduction in helping responses is less likely to occur in situations that are perceived to be dangerous, as opposed to non-dangerous. The authors suggested that this may be the case because there is less ambiguity surrounding dangerous situations, because the presence of other bystanders may reduce the fear of intervening, and because cooperation between bystanders may be more effective in resolving dangerous situations (Fischer et al., 2011).

In 1970, Latané and Darley introduced the situational model of bystander intervention. According to this model, there are five psychological steps that bystanders move through when deciding whether to intervene. The bystander must: (1) notice a critical situation; (2) construe the situation as an emergency; (3) develop a feeling of personal responsibility; (4) believe that they have the skills necessary to successfully intervene; and (5) reach a conscious decision to help (Latané & Darley, 1970). If there are situational barriers to any of the steps required, these can prevent the bystander from intervening. Piliavin et al. (1981) have since expanded on this model by introducing the 'arousal: cost-reward model'. Within this model, Piliavin et al. (1981) propose that if a situation arouses an emotional response in bystanders (i.e. empathy), they will be motivated to intervene. When experiencing these emotions, they may be motivated to alleviate the feelings by relieving the person/s directly impacted by the event of their distress via intervention (Piliavin et al., 1981; see also Dovidio et al., 1991, 2006; Voelpel et al., 2008; Wang, 2020). To do so, they assess the potential rewards (e.g. praise, compensation) versus the costs (e.g. personal harm, embarrassment) of intervening (Piliavin et al., 1981). In these circumstances, bystanders will seek to maximise the potential rewards and minimise the personal costs of intervening (Wang, 2020). For example, research has found that greater empathy and perceived likelihood of reward increase bystanders' preparedness to intervene in cyberbullying (Wang, 2020).

Research also suggests that prosocial tendencies reduce the perceived barriers to intervention and increase self-reported helping behaviours (Bennett et al., 2013). Contextual factors include the perceived severity of the situation, the relationship between the bystander and either the victim-survivor and/or the perpetrator, and feelings of social connectedness. For instance, greater perceived severity of the situation can increase the likelihood of bystander intervention (Fischer et al., 2011). Furthermore, the relationship to the victim-survivor may impact a person's likelihood of intervening, with some studies suggesting that people will express greater empathy and intention to intervene if the victim-survivor is a friend or someone they know (Bennett et al., 2017; Burn, 2009; Katz et al., 2015).

BYSTANDER INTERVENTION AND SEXUAL VIOLENCE

In more recent years, much of the available literature on bystander intervention has focused on sexual violence, particularly in university or college settings. Schwartz et al. (2001) proposed that sexual assault occurs when there is a motivated perpetrator, a potential victim-survivor, and the absence of 'capable guardians' or witnesses who could potentially intervene. While prevention efforts have largely focused on either perpetrators or victim-survivors (Burn, 2009), increasing attention has been paid to focusing on those capable guardians or bystanders.

There are a range of factors that influence whether people will intervene to disrupt sexual violence, as well as barriers that may prevent people from intervening. One of the most researched factors is the presence of other bystanders; however, a recent systematic review found that whether this acted to facilitate or hinder bystander intervention in the context of sexual violence remains unclear (Mainwaring et al., 2023). As outlined above, Latané and Darley (1970) identified five steps in determining whether a bystander will intervene in a critical incident. Burn (2009) conducted a study among undergraduate students at a Californian university to assess whether the barriers in the five-step situational model apply in cases of sexual assault. Findings from the survey provided some support for the model, with the five barriers being associated with reduced intervention behaviour, more so among men than women. However, McMahon and Banyard (2012) suggest that the application of Latané and Darley's (1970) model becomes complex in relation to sexual assault, because it may have different risk markers and patterns of behaviour compared to other critical events, such as medical emergencies.

Banyard (2011) used ecological models to expand knowledge on the factors that could promote or prevent bystanders from intervening when witnessing sexual violence. Banyard (2011) describes intrapersonal factors (i.e. factors within the individual) and contextual factors (i.e. factors outside the individual) that play a role in facilitating or preventing bystander intervention. Individual characteristics can include gender, personality, attitudes, and cognitions. There is, for example, evidence to suggest that women are more likely than men to intervene where they perceive there is a risk for sexual violence to occur (Banyard, 2008; Burn, 2009; Mainwaring et al., 2023). It is possible that this could be due to women's heightened awareness of sexual violence (Burn, 2009). Research has also found evidence to suggest that men are more likely than women to intervene to prevent sexual assault if the potential perpetrator is a friend, as opposed to a stranger (Burn, 2009). However, other studies have found the opposite to be the case, with people being more likely to report witnessing a crime, including sexual assault, if the perpetrator is a stranger (Bennett et al., 2017; Nicksa, 2014). Banyard (2008) found that people who had a greater sense of community also exhibited greater intentions to help and were more likely to engage in helping behaviours in sexual violence contexts.

Research suggests that the same individual and contextual factors that can facilitate bystander intervention can act as barriers to impede a person from intervening when witnessing sexual violence. Individual characteristics can include self-perceived skills to intervene, concerns around the repercussions of intervening, and problematic attitudes that people may hold around sexual and gender-based violence. In a study by Kania and Cale (2018) among university students in Australia, barriers to intervention included a failure to recognise the situation as high risk due to ignorance of the warning signs of sexual violence, as well as a failure to notice the situation. Furthermore, a study by Bennett et al. (2013) found that participants reported self-perceived skill deficits and a failure to take responsibility for intervening to be key barriers among college students in the United States. Fear of negative evaluation or 'evaluation apprehension' can act as a barrier to intervention, including concerns that others will view intervention as unnecessary or inappropriate (Burn, 2009). Acceptance of rape myths—that is, stereotypical or prejudiced beliefs about sexual violence, victim-survivors, and perpetrators—has also been consistently shown to be associated with a lower level of willingness to intervene among bystanders (Banyard, 2008; Banyard et al., 2007; Burgin & Flynn, 2021; McMahon, 2010), and lower rates of actual bystander intervention behaviour (Banyard, 2008; Banyard et al., 2007). Research indicates that men tend to be more accepting of rape myths compared to women (e.g. see Banyard, 2008; Banyard et al., 2007), and may express lower levels of willingness to intervene, as well as lower levels of actual intervention behaviour (Kania & Cale, 2018). This may go some way to explaining the gendered differences in intervention among men and women in sexual violence contexts.

Contextual factors might include perceptions of other bystanders' likelihood of supporting intervention. Specifically, there may be discrepancies between perceived and actual norms around bystander intervention, known as pluralistic ignorance (Brown & Messman-Moore,

2010; Fabiano et al., 2003; Kroshus, 2018). For example, Fabiano and colleagues (2003) found evidence to suggest that men hold misconceptions about their peers' level of support for intervening in instances of gender-based and sexual violence, perceiving that their peers would be less likely to support intervention than they are in reality. Such misconceptions can adversely influence intervention behaviours, over and above individual attitudes towards sexual violence. For instance, Brown and Messman-Moore (2010) found that male students' perceptions of the attitudes of their peers predicted willingness to intervene more than their own attitudes. To test this theory, Kroshus (2018) conducted a study examining pluralistic ignorance among college athletes and found that participants perceived that their teammates would be less supportive of intervening than they were, and these perceptions predicted participants' actual behaviours. These findings highlight the need for programs to improve awareness and capacity of bystanders to intervene when witnessing sexual violence.

Bystander Intervention Programs to Disrupt Sexual Violence

Bystander intervention programs are interventions that specifically seek to train peers or members of the community to identify the warning signs of violence—particularly sexual violence—and to intervene to prevent or disrupt it when it occurs (Kettrey & Marx, 2019a). These programs aim to provide people with the necessary attitudes, confidence, and skills to intervene (Banyard et al., 2007). Bystander intervention programs are increasingly being introduced and studied as a potential tool in violence prevention. By changing attitudes (such as reducing rape myth acceptance and increasing empathic concern for victim-survivors), these programs seek to foster a sense of personal responsibility to intervene. Such programs tend to adopt a community-focused approach to the prevention of sexual violence, by giving community members a specific role to play in the prevention of harm (Banyard et al., 2007).

A range of intervention programs have been introduced to foster prosocial bystander attitudes and behaviours in the context of sexual violence. Many of these have been introduced in university or college settings, given the extensive interest in bystander intervention in these contexts. For example, 'Bringing in the Bystander', which was developed by a team of researchers at the Prevention Innovations Research

Center, University of New Hampshire, is a multi-session program facilitated by a two-person team and delivered to single-sex or co-ed groups of students. Three 90-minute sessions provide participants with information about the role of bystanders within their communities, and teach students about appropriate and safe ways to intervene. Another example is 'Green Dot', a program which was originally developed for a student audience but has since been expanded to workplace and community contexts. The full program comprises four 'doses', where participants learn to recognise green dots (i.e. behaviours that promote safety) and red dots (i.e. behaviours that may contribute to violence). The program ultimately encourages participants to engage in more green dot behaviours to promote safety and disrupt violence in their community. Both the Bringing in the Bystander and Green Dot programs have been evaluated in a range of contexts, with evidence to support their efficacy in promoting prosocial bystander behaviour (Cares et al., 2015; Coker et al., 2011, 2014; Moynihan et al., 2011).

There have been several systematic or other reviews (DeGue et al., 2014; Evans et al., 2019; Mujal et al., 2019) and meta-analyses (Anderson & Whiston, 2005; Fenton et al., 2016; Jouriles et al., 2018; Katz & Moore, 2013; Kettrey & Marx, 2019a, 2019b; Kettrey et al., 2019) of bystander intervention programs related to sexual violence. Given that many of the existing bystander intervention programs focus on college students, the strongest evidence as to the effectiveness of bystander intervention programs in changing attitudes and behaviours relates to the university setting. Katz and Moore (2013) conducted one of the earliest systematic reviews of the effectiveness of programs for preventing sexual violence in college communities. Data from 12 studies among college students suggested that bystander intervention programs have positive effects on bystander attitudes (reducing rape-supportive attitudes), bystander efficacy (perceived competence in responding to sexual violence), intentions to intervene, and actual intervention behaviour. Their findings also indicated, however, that programs are more effective in improving bystander efficacy and intention to intervene, rather than actual bystander behaviour (Katz & Moore, 2013).

Kettrey and Marx (2019a) extended this idea in their systematic review examining the effects of bystander intervention programs on bystander efficacy, intentions, and bystander behaviour, and considered whether the moderating effects on these three factors differed depending on the timing of the program—implementation during the early or the later years of college. The rationale was that most college sexual assaults occur during the first two years of college (Cranney, 2015), suggesting that bystander intervention programs would be most effective if run during the earlier college years. Similar to Katz and Moore (2013), Kettrey and Marx (2019a) found that bystander intervention programs had positive effects on bystander efficacy, intentions, and behaviour. Furthermore, moderation analyses revealed that program effects on bystander intentions were significantly stronger in the early college years compared to the later college years, but the same did not hold for bystander efficacy or behaviour. The authors concluded that the timing of intervention may be important for encouraging greater intention to intervene among college students, but may not impact actual intervention behaviour (Kettrey & Marx, 2019a, 2019b).

Jouriles et al. (2018) conducted a systematic review of bystander intervention programs in college campuses with the aim of examining the impacts of the program on student attitudes, beliefs, and bystander behaviours. They found that students who participated in bystander intervention programs had more prosocial attitudes and beliefs around sexual violence and reported greater engagement in bystander behaviour. However, the effects of bystander intervention programs diminished over time, suggesting that repeated program engagement may have longer-term benefits in relation to bystander attitudes and behaviours (Jouriles et al., 2018). Finally, Mujal and colleagues (2019) conducted a systematic review of bystander intervention research for the prevention of sexual violence in the United States and Canada. Beyond expanding knowledge of the effectiveness of bystander intervention programs, the authors sought to identify the limitations of these studies. Of the 44 studies included in the review, a third included measurement of bystander behaviour after the intervention, with most reporting beneficial outcomes in relation to bystander attitudes (rape myth acceptance, sexist attitudes), confidence, self-efficacy, perceptions of denial and responsibility, and bystander behaviour. However, the authors reported several limitations of the bystander intervention evaluation studies in determining causality, including the use of quasi-experimental designs and limited follow-ups over time.

Bystander Intervention
and Image-Based Sexual Abuse

As others have noted, bystander intervention in the context of image-based sexual abuse presents unique contextual factors that may shape bystander intervention, including the potential broader reach and disparate locations of bystanders (Allison & Bussey, 2016; Krieger, 2020). Research suggests that bystanders have the potential to disrupt image-based sexual abuse behaviours and harms or prevent them from occurring (Barlińska et al., 2013; Brochado et al., 2017; Kowalski et al., 2014; Rebollo-Catalan & Mayor-Buzon, 2020; Song & Oh, 2018). However, there is limited evidence on the extent to which people witness or are bystanders to image-based sexual abuse. The Office of the eSafety Commissioner (2017) conducted a nationally representative survey of Australians to ascertain experiences, including bystander experiences, of image-based sexual abuse. Among a sample of more than 4,000 Australians, nearly one in five reported having been bystanders to image-based sexual abuse, including situations where they had received a nude or sexual photo and knew there was no consent, or were unsure of whether there was consent. Among these, four in ten did not take action in response (Office of the eSafety Commissioner, 2017). This corresponds with research that has examined people's perceptions of whether they would intervene in hypothetical scenarios of witnessing image-based sexual abuse. Powell et al. (2020) surveyed 6,109 participants across Australia, New Zealand, and the United Kingdom about experiences and perpetration of image-based sexual abuse. Participants were asked a series of questions to ascertain whether they would potentially intervene when witnessing image-based sexual abuse. Of their participants, 68% reported that they would say or do something to indicate their disapproval, or would like to say or do something (but did not know how). However, among participants who had witnessed image-based sexual abuse and reported having the opportunity to intervene, only 46% said that they did so (Powell et al., 2020). Women were more likely than men to report that they would say or do something in a hypothetical scenario, and that they had intervened when witnessing actual image-based sexual abuse (Powell et al., 2020).

Very few studies have examined how people feel towards image-based sexual abuse or the factors that may act to facilitate or act as a barrier to bystander intervention in the context of image-based sexual abuse. There is some evidence that people may judge image-based sexual abuse more leniently compared to physical sexual violence (Gibbard & Fido, 2023), suggesting that people may minimise or trivialise this form of harm. Although much of the research indicates that people express empathy and compassion towards victim-survivors, and perceive perpetrators of image-based sexual abuse to be highly blameworthy and deserving of criminal justice intervention, there is research demonstrating that victim-survivors may be blamed, particularly where the images were self-taken (Attrill-Smith et al., 2021; Flynn et al., 2023a; Zvi & Bitton, 2020). Where images have been self-taken, research has found that this may be a barrier to intervention towards both the victim-survivor and perpetrator (Mainwaring, 2023). Such attributions of blame tend to be higher among men compared to women (Attrill-Smith et al., 2021; Bothamley & Tully, 2018; Flynn et al., 2023a; Krieger, 2020; Zvi & Bitton, 2020), with men also reporting lower levels of empathy (Fido et al., 2021). These attributions of blame can impact perceptions of deserved punishment for perpetrators of image-based sexual abuse (Lageson et al., 2019; Zvi & Bitton, 2020), with men reporting more lenient perceptions of judgement towards perpetrators (Fido et al., 2021). Furthermore, perceptions of blame towards victim-survivors may impact whether people report that they would intervene in cases of image-based sexual abuse. Research by Pacilli and colleagues (2024) among the general Italian population, found that depictions of a victim-survivor with high sexual agency decreased survey participants' intentions of helping the victim-survivor, such as by reporting to the police or providing the victim-survivor with support and assistance. The research also found that depictions of a transient (compared to steady) relationship between the victim-survivor and perpetrator reduced intentions to help the victim-survivor, mediated by perceived moral virtue, and increased blame for image-based sexual abuse occurring.

In focus groups conducted in the United Kingdom, Mainwaring et al. (2024) found that the perceived likelihood of intervention increased where participants experienced greater feelings of responsibility, empathy with the victim-survivor, feelings of safety, and perceptions of greater benefits of police involvement. They also found that participants perceived a greater likelihood of intervention where they had reduced feelings of audience inhibition, greater anger towards the image-based sexual abuse behaviour, closer relationships with the victim-survivor or perpetrator, and where the image-based sexual abuse incident involved a female victim-survivor and a male perpetrator. In the same focus groups, participants described a range of actions they might take when witnessing image-based sexual abuse, including supporting the victim-survivor, directly or subtly taking action against the perpetrator, and taking justice-related actions, such as collecting evidence of the abuse or encouraging the victim-survivor to report to the police (Mainwaring et al., 2023).

Taken together, the data highlighted above underscore the need for further research on image-based sexual abuse and bystander intervention, including the barriers and facilitators to intervention. In the next section, we provide an overview of the chapters in this book which go some way towards addressing this research need.

Chapter Outline

The current study seeks to add to the limited literature on bystander intervention and image-based sexual abuse by examining bystanders' attitudes and willingness to intervene when witnessing image-based sexual abuse, and identifying the key influencing factors for bystanders, including the barriers and facilitators to intervention.

Chapter 2: The Image-Based Sexual Abuse and Bystander Intervention Study details the study methodology, including the aims and research questions, how the participants were recruited, and details on the survey and focus group questions, which involved posing a series of hypothetical scenarios on image-based sexual abuse and asking participants about whether and how they might intervene.

Chapter 3: Attitudes Towards Image-Based Sexual Abuse explores concepts of blame relating to image-based sexual abuse to shed light on attitudes towards these harms, and how these attitudes may shape or impact bystanders' intentions, readiness, and capacity to intervene. We draw comparisons between the survey and focus group data, and detail the demographic differences in attitudes, with a specific focus on gender (as this was a key variable in both the survey and focus group data). This chapter also focuses on the concept of victim-blaming in relation to image-based sexual abuse, including how focus group participants assigned blame and responsibility to aspects of the victim-survivor's behaviour and actions. We unpack nuances of the scenarios presented to participants, including how varying the victim-survivor and perpetrator gender in the scenarios presented played a role in influencing how participants attributed blame and harm.

Chapter 4: Time to Take Action: Barriers and Facilitators reports on the survey and focus group data findings relating to actual and perceived experiences of bystander intervention in image-based sexual abuse contexts. This includes detailing findings around whether participants reported having ever witnessed image-based sexual abuse, and if so, whether they said or did anything (and details of what they did/said, where relevant). We describe the motivations behind taking action or not taking action reported in the survey, and draw on the focus group data and hypothetical scenarios to describe common barriers to, and facilitators of, bystander intervention. In this chapter, we also explore participants' knowledge and beliefs regarding image-based sexual abuse laws, and whether this impacts on their likelihood to intervene when witnessing image-based sexual abuse incidents.

Chapter 5: The Role of Gender in Bystander Intervention examines the significant role that gender played in how and whether participants would intervene, including shaping attitudes towards the victim-survivor and perpetrator. We also explore how different gendered assumptions and expectations influence decision-making in bystander contexts.

Chapter 6: Bystanders and Image-Based Sexual Abuse: A Conclusion is the final chapter where we bring together the key themes to emerge from the study. This concluding chapter shines light on the new and ongoing challenges surrounding the prevention of image-based sexual abuse, and reflects on the importance of empowering bystanders to take action in response to image-based sexual abuse. It also outlines limitations of the study and proposes a future research agenda for scholars, researchers, and students working in this area.

Conclusion

This chapter has summarised the key definitions and literature relevant to image-based sexual abuse, including its prevalence, nature, and impacts. We have also conceptualised bystander intervention and presented a brief overview of existing literature on bystander interventions and their effectiveness. Finally, we provided an outline of the chapters to follow. The next chapter presents the study methodology, before moving onto a discussion of the findings.

REFERENCES

ABC. (2024, June 21). Sydney bartender Andrew Hayler jailed after sharing digitally altered images of women on porn site. *ABC News*. https://www.abc. net.au/news/2024-06-21/nsw-bartender-jailed-sharing-fake-images-women-on-porn-site/104005942

Allison, K. R., & Bussey, K. (2016). Cyber-bystanding in context: A review of the literature on witnesses' responses to cyberbullying. *Children and Youth Services Review, 65*, 183–194. https://doi.org/10.1016/j.childyouth.2016. 03.026

Anderson, L. A., & Whiston, S. C. (2005). Sexual assault education programs: A meta-analytic examination of their effectiveness. *Psychology of Women Quarterly, 29*(4), 374–388. https://doi.org/10.1111/j.1471-6402.2005.00237.x

Attrill-Smith, A., Wesson, C. J., Chater, M. L., & Weekes, L. (2021). Gender differences in videoed accounts of victim blaming for revenge porn for self-taken and stealth-taken sexually explicit images and videos. *Cyberpsychology: Journal of Psychosocial Research on Cyberspace, 15*(4), Article 3. https://doi. org/10.5817/CP2021-4-3

Barlińska, J., Szuster, A., & Winiewski, M. (2013). Cyberbullying among adolescent bystanders: Role of the communication medium, form of violence, and empathy. *Journal of Community & Applied Social Psychology., 23*(1), 37–51. https://doi.org/10.1002/casp.2137

Bailey, J., Flynn, A., & Henry, N. (2021). *The emerald international handbook of technology-facilitated violence and abuse*. Emerald Publishing.

Blais, J., McArthur, J. L., & Goruk, K. J. (2024). An examination of technology-facilitated sexual violence perpetration in Canada among a large sample of adults. *Canadian Journal of Behavioural Science / Revue canadienne des sciences du comportement. Advance online publication*. https://doi.org/10. 1037/cbs0000416

Banyard, V. L. (2008). Measurement and correlates of prosocial bystander behavior: The case of interpersonal violence. *Violence and Victims, 23*(1), 83–97. https://doi.org/10.1891/0886-6708.23.1.83

Banyard, V. L. (2011). Who will help prevent sexual violence: Creating an ecological model of bystander intervention. *Psychology of Violence, 1*(3), 216–229. https://doi.org/10.1037/a0023739

Banyard, V. L., Moynihan, M. M., & Plante, E. G. (2007). Sexual violence prevention through bystander education: An experimental evaluation. *Journal of Community Psychology, 35*(4), 463–481. https://or.g/1002/jcop.20159

Bates, S. (2017). Revenge porn and mental health: A qualitative analysis of the mental health effects of revenge porn on female survivors. *Feminist Criminology, 12*(1), 22–42. https://doi.org/10.1177/1557085116654565

Bennett, S., Banyard, V. L., & Edwards, K. M. (2017). The impact of the bystander's relationship with the victim and the perpetrator on intent to help in situations involving sexual violence. *Journal of Interpersonal Violence, 32*(5), 682–702. https://doi.org/10.1177/0886260515586373

Bennett, S., Banyard, V. L., & Garnhart, L. (2013). To act or not to act, that is the question? Barriers and facilitators of bystander intervention. *Journal of Interpersonal Violence, 29*(3), 476–496. https://doi.org/10.1177/088626 0513505210

Bond, E., & Tyrell, E. (2021). Understanding revenge pornography: A national survey of police officers and staff in England and Wales. *Journal of Interpersonal Violence, 36*(5–6), 2166–2181. https://doi.org/10.1177/086626051 8760011

Bothamley, S., & Tully, R. J. (2018). Understanding revenge pornography: Public perceptions of revenge pornography and victim-blaming. *Journal of Aggression, Conflict and Peace Research, 10*(1), 1–10. https://doi.org/10. 1108/JACPR-09-2016-0253

Brochado, S., Soares, S., & Fraga, S. (2017). A scoping review on studies of cyberbullying prevalence among adolescents. *Trauma, Violence, & Abuse, 18*(5), 523–531. https://doi.org/10.1177/1524838016641668

Brown, A. L., & Messman-Moore, T. L. (2010). Personal and perceived peer attitudes supporting sexual aggression as predictors of male college students' willingness to intervene against sexual aggression. *Journal of Interpersonal Violence, 25*(3), 503–517. https://doi.org/10.1177/0886260509334400

Burgin, R., & Flynn, A. (2021). Women's behavior as implied consent: Male "reasonableness" in Australian rape law. *Criminology & Criminal Justice, 21*(3), 334–352. https://doi.org/10.1177/1748895819880953

Burn, S. M. (2009). A situational model of sexual assault prevention through bystander intervention. *Sex Roles: A Journal of Research, 60*(11–12), 779–792. https://doi.org/10.1007/s11199-008-9581-5

Cama, E. (2021). Understanding experiences of sexual harms facilitated through dating and hook up apps among women and girls. In J. Bailey, A. Flynn, & N. Henry (Eds.), *The emerald international handbook of technology-facilitated violence and abuse* (pp. 333–350). Emerald Publishing.

Cares, A. C., Banyard, V. L., Moynihan, M. M., Williams, L. M., Potter, S. J., & Stapleton, J. G. (2015). Changing attitudes about being a bystander to violence: Translating an in-person education program to a new campus. *Violence Against Women, 21*(2), 165–187. https://doi.org/10.1177/107780 1214564681

Champion, A. R., Oswald, F., Khera, D., & Pederson, C. L. (2022). Examining the gendered impacts of technology-facilitated sexual violence: A mixed methods approach. *Archival Sexual Behaviour, 51*(3), 1607–1624. https:// doi.org/10.1007/s10508-021-02226-y

Chalton, A., & Schollum, P. (2020). *Sentencing image-based sexual abuse offences in Victoria*. Sentencing Advisory Council. Retrieved October 21,

2024, from https://www.sentencingcouncil.vic.gov.au/sites/default/files/2020-10/Sentencing_Image_Based_Sexual_Abuse_Offences_in_Victoria.pdf

Citron, D. K., & Franks, M. A. (2014). Criminalizing revenge porn. *Wake Forest Law Review, 49*(2), 345391.

Clarke, D. (2003). *Pro-social and anti-social behaviour.* Routledge.

Coker, A. L., Cook-Craig, P. G., Williams, C. M., Fisher, B. S., Clear, E. R., Garcia, L. S., & Hegge, L. M. (2011). Evaluation of Green Dot: An active bystander intervention to reduce sexual violence on college campuses. *Violence against Women, 17*(6), 777–796. https://doi.org/10.1177/1077801211410264

Coker, A. L., Fisher, B. S., Bush, H. M., Swan, S. C., Williams, C. M., Clear, E. R., & DeGue, S. (2014). Evaluation of the Green Dot bystander intervention to reduce interpersonal violence among college students across three campuses. *Violence against Women, 21*(12), 1507–1527. https://doi.org/10.1177/1077801214545284

Cranney, S. (2015). The relationship between sexual victimization and year in school in U.S. colleges: Investigating the parameters of the 'red zone'. *Journal of Interpersonal Violence, 30*(17), 3133–3145. https://doi.org/10.1177/0886260514554425

Criminal Code Act 1995 (Cth)

Criminal Code Amendment (Deepfake Sexual Material Bill 2024 (Cth)

Cyber Civil Rights Initiative. (2014). *End revenge porn: A campaign of the Cyber Civil Rights Initiative.* Retrieved October 21, 2024, from https://www.cybercivilrights.org/wp-content/uploads/2014/12/RPStatistics.pdf

Darley, J. M., & Latané, B. (1968). Bystander intervention in emergencies: Diffusion of responsibility. *Journal of Personality and Social Psychology, 8*(4, Pt. 1), 377–383. https://doi.org/10.1037/h0025589

DeGue, S., Valle, L. A., Holt, M. K., Massetti, G. M., Matjasko, J. L., & Tharp, A. T. (2014). A systematic review of primary prevention strategies for sexual violence perpetration. *Aggression and Violent Behavior, 19*(4), 346–362. https://doi.org/10.1016/j.avb.2014.05.004

Dovidio, J. F., Piliavin, J. A., Gaertner, S. L., Schroeder, D. A., & Clark, R. D. (1991). The arousal: Cost-reward model and the process of intervention—A review of the evidence. *Review of Personality and Social Psychology, 12*, 86–118.

Dovidio, J. F., Piliavin, J. A., Schroeder, D. A., & Penner, L. A. (2006). *The social psychology of prosocial behavior.* Lawrence, Erlbaum. *Bulletin, 100*(3), 283–308. https://doi.org/10.1037/0033-2909.100.3.283

Eaton, A. A., Jacobs, H., & Ruvalcaba, Y. (2018). *2017 nationwide online study of non-consensual porn victimization and perpetration: A summary report.* Retrieved October 21, 2024, from https://www.cybercivilrights.org/wp-content/uploads/2017/06/CCRI-2017-Research-Report.pdf

Evans, J. L., Burroughs, M. E., & Knowlden, A. P. (2019). Examining the efficacy of bystander sexual violence interventions for first-year college students:
A systematic review. *Aggression and Violent Behavior, 48*, 72–82. https://doi.
org/10.1016/j.avb.2019.08.016

Fabiano, P. M., Perkins, H. W., Berkowitz, A., Linkenbach, J., & Stark, C.
(2003). Engaging men as social justice allies in ending violence against
women: Evidence for a social norms approach. *Journal of American College
Health, 52*(3), 105–112. https://doi.org/10.1080/0744848030959573

Fenton, R. A., Mott, H. L., McCartan, K., & Rumney, P. (2016). *A review of
evidence for bystander intervention to prevent sexual and domestic violence in
universities.* Retrieved October 24, 2024, from https://assets.publishing.ser
vice.gov.uk/media/5a802686ed915d74e622cc3b/Evidence_review_bystan
der_intervention_to_prevent_sexual_and_domestic_violence_in_universities_
11April2016.pdf

Fido, D., Harper, C. A., Davis, M. A., Petronzi, D., & Worrall, S. (2021).
Intrasexual competition as a predictor of women's judgments of revenge
pornography offending. *Sexual Abuse, 33*(3), 295–320. https://doi-org.www
proxy1.library.unsw.edu.au/10.1177/1079063219894306

Fischer, P., Krueger, J., Greitemeyer, T., Vogrincic, C., Kastenmüller, A., Frey,
D., Heene, M., Wicher, M., & Kainbacher, M. (2011). The bystander-effect:
A meta-analytic review on bystander intervention in dangerous and non-
dangerous emergencies. *Psychological Bulletin, 137*(4), 517–537. https://doi.
org/10.1037/a0023304

Flynn, A. (2023). Image-based sexual abuse. In H. Pontell (Ed.), *Oxford research
encyclopedia of criminology and criminal justice* (2nd ed.). Oxford University
Press. https://doi.org/10.1093/acrefore/9780190264079.013.534

Flynn, A., Cama, E., Powell, A., & Scott, A. J. (2023a). Victim-blaming and
image-based sexual abuse. *Journal of Criminology, 56*(1), 7–15. https://doi.
org/10.1177/26338076221135327

Flynn, A., Clough, J., & Cooke, T. (2022a). Disrupting and preventing deepfake
abuse: Exploring criminal law responses to AI Facilitated Abuse. In A. Powell,
A. Flynn, & L. Sugiura (Eds.), *The Palgrave handbook of gendered violence and
technology* (pp. 583–602). Palgrave Macmillan.

Flynn, A., & Henry, N. (2021). Image-based sexual abuse: An Australian reflection. *Women and Criminal Justice, 31*(4), 313–326. https://doi.org/10.
1080/08974454.2019.1646190

Flynn, A., Scott, A. J., & Cama, E. (2024a). An empirical research study
on barriers, facilitators, and strategies to promote bystander intervention in
intimate image abuse contexts. In K. Summerer & G. M. Caletti (Eds.),
Criminalising intimate image abuse (pp. 376–399). Oxford University Press.

Flynn, A., Powell, A., Eaton, A., & Scott, A. J. (2024b, April 3). Legal loopholes don't help victims of sexualised deepfake abuse. *360info*. https://360info. org/legal-loopholes-dont-help-victims-of-sexualised-deepfake-abuse/

Flynn, A., Powell, A., & Hindes, S. (2023b). Policing technology–facilitated abuse. *Policing & Society, 33*(5), 572–592. https://doi.org/10.1080/104 39463.2022.2159400

Flynn, A., Powell, A., & Hindes, S. (2024c). An intersectional analysis of technology-facilitated abuse: Prevalence, experiences and impacts of victimization. *British Journal of Criminology, 64*(3), 600–619. https://doi.org/10. 1093/bjc/azad044

Flynn, A., Powell, A., Scott, A. J., & Cama, E. (2022b). Deepfakes and digitally altered imagery abuse: A cross-country exploration of an emerging form of image-based sexual abuse. *British Journal of Criminology, 62*(6), 1341–1358. https://doi.org/10/1093.bjc/azab111

Franks, M. A. (2017). 'Revenge porn' reform: A view from the front lines. *Florida Law Review, 69,* 1252–1337.

Gibbard, G., & Fido, D. (2023). A comparison of judgements of image-based and physical sexual abuse: A pilot study. *Journal of Concurrent Disorders, 5*(1), 92–102. https://doi.org/10.54127/UPKC8347

Goujard, C. (2024, February 6). Taylor Swift deepfakes nudge EU to get real about AI. *Politico*. https://www.politico.eu/article/europe-eye-fix-taylor-swift-nude-deepfake/

Gordon-Messer, D., Bauermeister, J., Grodziniski, A., & Zimmerman, M. (2013). Sexting among young adults. *Journal of Adolescent Health, 52*(3), 301–306. https://doi.org/10.1016/j.jadohealth.2012.05.013

Henry, N., & Beard, G. (2024). Image-based sexual abuse perpetration: A scoping review. *Trauma, Violence, & Abuse.* Advanced online publication. https://doi.org/10.1177/15248380241266137

Henry, N., Flynn, A., & Powell, A. (2018). Policing image-based sexual abuse: Stakeholder perspectives. *Police Practice and Research: An International Journal, 19*(6), 565–581. https://doi.org/10.1080/15614263.2018. 1507892

Henry, N., Flynn, A., & Powell, A. (2019a). *Responding to revenge pornography: The scope, nature and impact of Australian criminal laws—A report to the Criminology Research Council.* Australian Institute of Criminology. Retrieved October 21, 2024, from https://www.aic.gov.au/sites/default/files/2020-05/CRG_08_15-16-FinalReport.pdf

Henry, N., Flynn, A., & Powell, A. (2019b). Image-based sexual abuse: Victims and perpetrators. *Trends & Issues in Crime and Justice, 572,* 1–19. https://doi.org/10.52922/ti09975

Henry, N., McGlynn, C., Flynn, A., Johnson, K., Powell, A., & Scott, A. J. (2020). *Image-based sexual abuse: A study on the causes and consequences of non-consensual nude or sexual imagery*. Routledge.

Jouriles, E. N., Krauss, A., Vu, N. L., Banyard, V. L., & McDonald, R. (2018). Bystander programs addressing sexual violence on college campuses: A systematic review and meta-analysis of program outcomes and delivery methods. *Journal of American College Health, 66*(6), 457–466. https://doi.org/10.1080/07448481.2018.1431906

Kania, R., & Cale, J. (2018). Preventing sexual violence through bystander intervention: Attitudes, behaviors, missed opportunities, and barriers to intervention among Australian university students. *Journal of Interpersonal Violence, 36*(5–6), 2816–2840. https://doi.org/10.1177/0886260518764395

Katz, J., & Moore, J. (2013). Bystander education training for campus sexual assault prevention: An initial meta-analysis. *Violence and Victims, 28*(6), 1054–1067. https://doi.org/10.1891/0886-6708.vv-d-12-00113

Katz, J., Pazienza, R., Olin, R., & Rich, H. (2015). That's what friends are for: Bystander responses to friends or strangers at risk for party rape victimization. *Journal of Interpersonal Violence, 30*(16), 2775–2792. https://doi.org/10.1177/0886260514554290

Kettrey, H. H., & Marx, R. A. (2019a). The effects of bystander programs on the prevention of sexual assault across the college years: A systematic review and meta-analysis. *Journal of Youth and Adolescence, 48*, 212–227. https://doi.org/10.1007/s10964-018-0927-1

Kettrey, H. H., & Marx, R. A. (2019b). Does the gendered approach of bystander programs matter in the prevention of sexual assault among adolescents and college students? A systematic review and meta-analysis. *Archives of Sexual Behavior, 48*, 2037–2053. https://doi.org/10.1007/s10508-019-01503-1

Kettrey, H. H., Marx, R. A., & Tanner-Smith, E. E. (2019). Effects of bystander programs on the prevention of sexual assault among adolescents and college students: A systematic review. *Campbell Systematic Reviews, 15*(1–2), e1013. https://doi.org/10.4073/csr.2019.1

Kirchengast, T. (2020). Deepfakes and image manipulation: Criminalisation and control. *Information & Communications Technology Law, 29*(3), 308–323. https://doi.org/10.1080/13600834.2020.1794615

Kowalski, R., Giumetti, G., Schroeder, A., & Lattanner, M. (2014). Bullying in the digital age: A critical review and meta-analysis of cyberbullying research among youth. *Psychological Bulletin, 140*(4), 1073–1137. https://doi.org/10.1037/a0035618

Krieger, M. A. (2020). *Image-based sexual violence: Victim experiences and bystander responses* (Doctoral thesis). Department of Psychology, University of Windsor. Scholarship at UWindsor. https://scholar.uwindsor.ca/etd/8335

Kroshus, E. (2018). College athletes, pluralistic ignorance and bystander behaviors to prevent sexual assault. *Journal of Clinical Sport Psychology, 13*(2), 330–344. https://doi.org/10.1123/jcsp.2018-0039

Lageson, S. E., McElrath, S., & Palmer, K. E. (2019). Gendered public support for criminalizing "revenge porn." *Feminist Criminology, 14*(5), 560–583. https://doi.org/10.1177/1557085118773398

Latané, B., & Darley, J. M. (1970). *The unresponsive bystander: Why doesn't he help?* Appleton-Century-Croft.

Lenhart, A., Ybarra, M., & Price-Feeney, M. (2016). *Non-consensual image sharing: One in 25 Americans has been a victim of 'revenge porn'.* Data and Society Research Institute and Center for Innovative Public Health Research. Retrieved October 21, 2024, from from https://datasociety.net/pubs/oh/Nonconsensual_Image_Sharing_2016.pdf

Mainwaring, C. (2023). *An investigation into the role of individual, situational, and contextual facilitators and barriers of bystander intervention intent in image-based sexual abuse contexts* (Doctoral thesis). Goldsmiths, University of London. Goldsmiths Research Online. https://research.gold.ac.uk/id/eprint/33325/

Mainwaring, C., Scott, A. J., & Gabbert, F. (2023). Behavioral intentions of bystanders to image-based sexual abuse: A preliminary focus group study with a university student sample. *Journal of Child Sexual Abuse, 32*(3), 318–339. https://doi.org/10.1080/10538712.2023.2190734

Mainwaring, C., Scott, A. J., & Gabbert, F. (2024). Facilitators and barriers of bystander intervention intent in image-based sexual abuse contexts: A focus group study with a university sample. *Journal of Interpersonal Violence, 39*(11–12), 2655–2686. https://doi.org/10.1177/08862605231222452

McGlynn, C., Rackley, E., Johnson, K., Henry, N., Gavey, N., Flynn, A., & Powell, A. (2021). 'It's torture for the soul':' The harms of image-based sexual abuse. *Social & Legal Studies, 30*(4), 541–562. https://doi.org/10.1177/0964663920947791

McMahon, S. (2010). Rape myth beliefs and bystander attitudes among incoming college students. *Journal of American College Health, 59*(1), 3–11. https://doi.org/10.1080/07448481.2010.483715

McMahon, S., & Banyard, V. L. (2012). When can I help? A conceptual framework for the prevention of sexual violence through bystander intervention. *Trauma, Violence, & Abuse, 13*(1), 3–14. https://doi.org/10.1177/1524838011426015

Moynihan, M. M., Banyard, V. L., Arnold, J. S., Eckstein, R. P., & Stapleton, J. G. (2011). Sisterhood may be powerful for reducing sexual and intimate partner violence: An evaluation of the Bringing in the Bystander in-person program with sorority members. *Violence Against Women, 17*(6), 703–719. https://doi.org/10.1177/1077801211409726

Mujal, G. N., Taylor, M. E., Fry, J. L., Gochez-Kerr, T. H., & Weaver, N. L. (2019). A systematic review of bystander interventions for the prevention of sexual violence. *Trauma, Violence, & Abuse, 22*(2), 381–396. https://doi.org/10.1177/1524838019849587

NBC. (2024, January 28). Taylor Swift's name not searchable on X days after sexually explicit deepfakes go viral. *NBC News*. https://www.nbcnews.com/news/us-news/taylor-swifts-name-not-searchable-x-days-sexually-explicit-dee pfakes-g-rcna136017

Nicksa, S. C. (2014). Bystander's willingness to report theft, physical assault, and sexual assault: The impact of gender, anonymity, and relationship with the offender. *Journal of Interpersonal Violence, 29*(2), 217–236. https://doi.org/10.1177/0886260513505146

Office of the eSafety Commissioner. (2017). *Image-based abuse: National survey—Summary report*. Retrieved 21 October, 2024, from https://www.esafety.gov.au/about-us/research/image-based-abuse

Pacilli, M. G., Pagliaro, S., Giovannelli, I., Spaccatini, F., Berlin, E., & Rollero, C. (2024). *From non-traditional sexual behavior to non-legitimate victims: Moral virtue, victim blame, and helping intentions toward a woman victim of image-based sexual abuse*. Advanced online publication. https://doi.org/10.1007/s10508-024-02970-x

Paradiso, M. N., Rollè, L., & Trombetta, T. (2024). Image-based sexual abuse associated factors: A systematic review. *Journal of Family Violence, 39*, 931–954. https://doi.org/10.1007/s10896-023-00557-z

Patel, U., & Roesch, R. (2022). The prevalence of technology-facilitated sexual violence: A meta-analysis and systematic review. *Trauma, Violence, & Abuse, 23*(2), 428–443. https://doi.org/10.1177/1524838020

Pew Research Centre. (2021). *The state of online harassment*. Retrieved October 21, 2024, from https://www.pewresearch.org/wp-content/uploads/sites/20/2021/01/PI_2021.01.13_Online-Harassment_FINAL-1.pdf

Piliavin, J. A., Dovidio, J. F., Gaertner, S. L., & Clark, R. (1981). *Emergency intervention*. Academic Press.

Powell, A. (2011). *Review of bystander approaches in support of preventing violence against women*. Victorian Health Promotion Foundation (VicHealth).

Powell, A., & Flynn, A. (2023). Technology-facilitated abuse victimization: A gendered analysis in a representative survey of adults. *Feminist Criminology, 18*(5), 435–458. https://doi.org/10.1177/15570851231196548

Powell, A., Flynn, A., & Henry, N. (2019a). Sexual violence in digital society: Human, Technical and Social Factors. In T. Holt & R. Lukfeld (Eds.), *Understanding the human factor of cybercrime* (pp. 134–155). Routledge.

Powell, A., Flynn, A., & Hindes, S. (2022). *Technology-facilitated abuse: National survey of Australian adults' experiences* (Research report, 12/2022). ANROWS.

Powell, A., Henry, N., & Flynn, A. (2018). Image-based sexual abuse. In W. S. DeKeseredy, C. M. Rennison, & A. K. Hall-Sanchez (Eds.), *The Routledge international handbook of violence studies* (pp. 305–315). Routledge.

Powell, A., Henry, N., Flynn, A., & Scott, A. J. (2019b). Image-based sexual abuse: The extent, nature, and predictors of perpetration in a community sample of Australian adults. *Computers in Human Behavior, 92*, 393–402. https://doi.org/10.1016/j.chb.2018.11.009

Powell, A., Scott, A. J., Flynn, A., & Henry, N. (2020). *Image-based sexual abuse: An international study of victims and perpetrators*. RMIT University. Retrieved October 21, 2024, from https://www.researchgate.net/public ation/339488012_Image-based_sexual_abuse_An_international_study_of_v ictims_and_perpetrators

Powell, A., Scott, A. J., Flynn, A., & McCook, S. (2022b). A multi-country study of image-based sexual abuse: Extent, relational nature and correlates of victimisation experiences. *Journal of Sexual Aggression, 30*(1), 25–40. https://doi.org/10.1080/13552600.2022.2119292

Powell, A., Scott, A. J., Flynn, A., & McCook, S. (2022c). Perpetration of image-based sexual abuse: Extent, nature and correlates in a multi-country sample. *Journal of Interpersonal Violence, 37*(23–24), 22864–22889. https://doi.org/10.1177/08862605211072266

Rebollo-Catalan, A., & Mayor-Buzon, V. (2020). Adolescent bystanders witnessing cyber violence against women and girls: What they observe and how they respond. *Violence against Women, 26*(15–16), 2024–2040. https://doi.org/10.1177/1077801219888025

Ruvalcaba, Y., & Eaton, A. A. (2020). Nonconsensual pornography among U.S. adults: A sexual scripts framework on victimization, perpetration, and health correlates for women and men. *Psychology of Violence, 10*(1), 68–78. https://doi.org/10.1037/vio0000233

Schwartz, M. D., DeKeseredy, W. S., Tait, D., & Alvi, S. (2001). Male peer support and a feminist routine activities theory: Understanding sexual assault on the college campus. *Justice Quarterly, 18*(3), 623–649. https://doi.org/10.1080/07418820100095041

Snaychuk, L. A., & O'Neill, M. L. (2020). Technology-facilitated sexual violence: Prevalence, risk, and resiliency in undergraduate students. *Journal of Aggression, Maltreatment & Trauma, 29*(8), 984–999. https://doi.org/10.1080/10926771.2019.1710636

Song, J., & Oh, I. (2018). Factors influencing bystanders' behavioral reactions in cyberbullying situations. *Computers in Human Behavior, 78*, 273–282. https://doi.org/10.1016/j.chb.2017.10.008

Taket, A., & Crisp, B. R. (2017). *Bystanders for primary prevention: A rapid review*. VicHealth.

Umbach, R., Henry, N., Beard, G., & Berryessa, C. (2024). Non-consensual synthetic intimate imagery: Prevalence, attitudes, and knowledge in 10 countries. In *Proceedings of the CHI Conference on Human Factors in Computing Systems*, Article 779. https://doi.org/10.1145/3613904.3642382

VicHealth. (2011). *A technical report on the conduct and findings of VicHealth's survey of bystander knowledge, attitudes and behaviours in preventing violence against women.* VicHealth.

Voelpel, S. C., Eckhoff, R. A., & Forster, J. (2008). David against Goliath? Group size and bystander effects in virtual knowledge sharing. *Human Relations, 61*(2), 271–295. https://doi.org/10.1177/0018726707087787

Walker, K., & Sleath, E. (2017). A systematic review of the current knowledge regarding revenge pornography and non-consensual sharing of sexually explicit media. *Aggression and Violent Behavior, 36*, 9–24. https://doi.org/10.1016/j.avb.2017.06.010

Wang, S. (2020). Standing up or standing by: Bystander intervention in cyberbullying on social media. *New Media & Society, 23*(6), 1279–1397. https://doi.org/10.1177/1461444820902541

Woods, C. (2024, February 22). The spotlight cast by Taylor Swift's deepfake experience. *LSJ Online.* https://lsj.com.au/articles/the-spotlight-cast-by-taylor-swifts-deepfake-experience/

Zvi, L., & Bitton, M. S. (2020). Perceptions of victim and offender culpability in non-consensual distribution of intimate images. *Psychology, Crime & Law, 27*(5), 427–442. https://doi.org/10.1080/1068316X.2020.1818236

CHAPTER 2

The Image-Based Sexual Abuse and Bystander Intervention Study

Abstract This chapter outlines the study methodology for the Image-Based Abuse and Bystander Intervention Study, which is the first mixed methods study to focus specifically on bystander intervention in image-based sexual abuse contexts. This chapter presents the research questions, information about the sample, and how participants were recruited, as well as details on the survey and focus group questions. The study involved posing a series of hypothetical scenarios—outlined in this chapter—on image-based sexual abuse to participants and asking whether and how they might intervene.

Keywords Image-based sexual abuse · Bystander · Intervention · Survey · Focus groups

INTRODUCTION

The Image-Based Sexual Abuse and Bystander Intervention Study sought to better understand Australian's attitudes towards image-based sexual abuse, their knowledge of image-based sexual abuse laws and other avenues of victim-survivor support, and whether they would be prepared

© The Author(s), under exclusive license to Springer Nature
Switzerland AG 2025
A. Flynn et al., *Image-Based Sexual Abuse and Bystander Intervention*,
Palgrave Studies in Cybercrime and Cybersecurity,
https://doi.org/10.1007/978-3-031-83647-3_2

to intervene or take action when witnessing an image-based sexual abuse incident. Specifically, we sought to answer the following three questions:

1. What attitudes do Australians hold towards image-based sexual abuse?
2. How much do Australians know about the applicable laws and available responses to image-based sexual abuse?
3. How ready would Australians feel to intervene when they witness image-based sexual abuse, what actions would they take, and what factors influence their decisions?

To answer these questions, we conducted a mixed methods study involving surveys and focus groups with a cohort of Australians aged 18 to 71 years. Participants resided in four major capital cities in Australia: Adelaide (South Australia), Canberra (Australian Capital Territory), Melbourne (Victoria), and Sydney (New South Wales). As the project sought to test knowledge of image-based sexual abuse laws and responses, these locations were selected because image-based sexual abuse laws were in place at the time of conducting the research. Since the completion of the project, image-based sexual abuse laws have been introduced across all Australian jurisdictions, except for Tasmania, including at the federal level (see Flynn, 2023). Participants were asked to complete the anonymous online survey in advance of attending the focus groups (more details provided below). The project received ethics approval from the Monash University Human Research Ethics Committee (project number: 17905).

In this chapter, we outline the methodology, including the recruitment strategy, sample/setting, procedure/materials, and analysis approach.

Recruitment Strategy

Participants were recruited using cost-effective and efficient methods successfully adopted by members of the research team in previous studies (see Flynn et al., 2023; Powell et al., 2022a, 2022b). This included creating flyers advertising the focus groups and directing interested parties to a project Facebook page and a (now expired) project website. Members of the research team sent the digital flyers to their professional contacts among relevant stakeholders, community leaders, and academics, as well as relevant community organisations and groups whose members may have been interested in participating. Digital and hard copies of the flyer were also distributed across university campuses, Facebook group pages, and community noticeboards (e.g. local libraries, shopping centres), and posted on professional social media accounts. Paid Facebook advertising was used to assist with recruitment specifically targeting people based on their identified location in Adelaide, Canberra, Melbourne, or Sydney. The advertisements promoted the focus groups and directed potential participants to visit the project website.

The project website housed information regarding the research, including a copy of the explanatory statement describing what would be required of participants (e.g. complete an online anonymous survey and attend a one-hour in-person focus group), the details of the focus groups, including dates, times, and locations, a link to register interest in participating, and a contact email created specifically for the project. When someone registered their interest in the research, the information was sent to the project email, and a member of the research team responded to confirm the participant's preferred date, time, and location, as well as any dietary requirements.

Upon completing the survey, participants created a unique code based on their birth date, year, and initials. This unique identifier was used for a sign-in sheet for the focus groups to ensure the participant had completed the survey prior to attending the focus group. These records were deleted following completion of the focus groups and were not compared to the survey data.

SURVEY

Sample/Setting

Participants were asked to complete an anonymous survey hosted by Qualtrics XM in May and June 2019, prior to attending their preferred focus group. The survey sample comprised 245 Australian residents with an average age of 31.20 years (SD = 13.02, Range = 18 to 71 years). Most of the sample identified as female (65.7%), followed by male (29.8%), and non-binary, transgender, or other gender identity (4.5%). Regarding sexuality, most of the sample identified as heterosexual (74.7%), with the remaining sample identifying as lesbian (3.3%), gay

(4.9%), bisexual (11.8%), queer (2.0%), or other sexual identity (3.3%). Due to lower numbers among these individual categories, those identifying as lesbian, gay, bisexual, queer, or other sexual identity were grouped to form an LGQBI+ (25.3%) category for the purpose of statistical analyses (see Table 2.1 for additional demographic information).

Table 2.1   Demographic information

	Percentage	*Number*
Gender		
Female	65.7	161
Male	29.8	73
Non-binary, transgender, or other gender identity	4.5	11
Sexuality		
Heterosexual	74.7	183
LGBQI+	25.3	62
Ethnicity		
Asian	25.3	62
Mixed	6.9	17
White	58.8	144
Other	9.0	22
Languages spoken other than English		
No	73.5	180
Yes	26.5	65
Education		
Secondary/high school	32.7	80
Trade certificate	16.3	40
Undergraduate/postgraduate degree	50.2	123
Other	0.8	2
Employment status		
Full-time	20.8	51
Part-time	11.8	29
Student	35.6	87
Other	31.8	78
State of residence		
Australia Capital Territory (ACT)	14.3	35
New South Wales (NSW)	29.4	72
South Australia (SA)	27.3	67
Victoria (VIC)	29.0	71
Total	100.0	245

Procedure/Materials

The survey was adapted from existing international survey research (e.g. Cyber Civil Rights Initiative, 2014; Englander, 2015; McAfee, 2013), including that previously undertaken by members of the research team (see Henry et al., 2020; Powell et al., 2019). The survey included questions regarding attitudes towards image-based sexual abuse, experiences and perceptions of witnessing image-based sexual abuse, knowledge of image-based sexual abuse laws, and demographic characteristics. We used the term 'non-consensual imagery' to describe image-based sexual abuse behaviours throughout the survey and focus groups to avoid influencing or shaping attitudes and views of the behaviours described. However, we use the term 'image-based sexual abuse' throughout the book when reporting on the data from the survey and focus groups for consistency and clarity.

Attitudes towards intimate image sharing: Drawing from previous work by members of the research team (see, e.g., Powell et al., 2019, 2020a), participants were asked to indicate how strongly they agreed or disagreed with 36 statements relating to their attitudes towards a range of sexual, dating, and relationship behaviours involving nude or sexual images (see Table 2.2). They indicated their level of agreement via a seven-point scale (ranging from 1 'strongly disagree' to 7 'strongly agree'). As explained in the analysis approach section of this chapter, these statements were grouped into four components following principal components analysis: blame, acceptable exceptions, positive impact, and minimisation. A fifth category for items that were not assigned to one of these four components is also included below, although these items were excluded from subsequent statistical analyses.

Experiences witnessing image-based sexual abuse: Participants were asked whether they had witnessed or become aware of someone engaging in seven image-based sexual abuse behaviours: taking, sharing, uploading, threatening to share, downblousing, upskirting, and other (see Table 2.3). The seven questions were measured via a six-point scale (ranging from 'no' to '5+ times').

Most recent experience witnessing image-based sexual abuse: Participants who had witnessed image-based sexual abuse were asked about their most recent experience, including how they felt about it and whether they said or did anything in response. Participants indicated how strongly they experienced nine different feelings in response to their most

Table 2.2   Intimate image sharing statements

Blame

1. A man who sends a nude or sexual image to his partner, shouldn't be surprised if the image ends up online
2. If a man sends a nude or sexual image to a partner, he can't expect it to remain private
3. A person who sends a nude or sexual 'selfie' to another person is partly to blame if the image ends up online
4. If a person is willing to let their partner film them having sex, then they are partly to blame if that video ends up online
5. A woman who sends a nude or sexual image to her partner shouldn't be surprised if the image ends up online
6. People who share nude or sexual images of themselves with another person are partly to blame if the images are shown to others
7. If a woman sends a nude or sexual image to someone she just met, she shouldn't be surprised if the image ends up online
8. If a woman sends a nude or sexual image to a partner she can't expect it to remain private
9. People shouldn't take nude or sexual images of themselves if they do not want them to be shared with others
10. If a man sends a nude or sexual image to someone he just met, he shouldn't be surprised if the image ends up online
11. People should know better than to take nude selfies even if they never send them to anyone

Acceptable exceptions

12. It's okay for a person who receives a 'dick pic' (i.e. an image of a penis) they didn't want or ask for to show it to their friends
13. It's okay for a person who receives a 'twat shot' (i.e. an image of a vagina) they didn't want or ask for to show it to their friends
14. If a man is willing to send a nude or sexual image to someone he just met, then it's no big deal if they show it to their friends

Positive impact

15. A woman's reputation is boosted among her friends if she shares nude or sexual images of a sexual partner
16. A man's reputation is boosted among his friends if he shares nude or sexual images of a sexual partner
17. If a man shares a nude or sexual image of his partner with his friends, it just shows how proud he is of them
18. If a woman shares a nude or sexual image of her partner with her friends, it just shows how proud she is of them
19. Although most women wouldn't admit it, they find it a turn-on for their partner to share nude or sexual images of them with friends
20. Although most men wouldn't admit it, they find it a turn-on for their partner to share nude or sexual images of them with friends

---

(continued)

Table 2.2 (continued)

21. A man should be flattered if a partner or ex-partner shares nude or sexual images of him with some close friends

Minimisation

22. A woman shouldn't get upset if her partner shares nude or sexual images of her with others
23. It's not a big deal if a nude or sexual image of a gay man is shared without his permission
24. It's not a big deal if a topless image of a transgender woman is shared without her permission
25. It's not a big deal if a nude or sexual image of a lesbian woman is shared without her permission
26. A woman should be flattered if a partner or ex-partner shares nude or sexual images of her with some close friends
27. If a man shares a nude or sexual image of his partner with his friends when he's drunk, he can't really be held responsible
28. A man shouldn't get upset if his partner shares nude or sexual images of him with others
29. Women tend to exaggerate the impact of having a nude or sexual image of themselves shared without their permission
30. If a woman shares a nude or sexual image of her partner with her friends when she's drunk, she can't really be held responsible

Non-assigned

31. It's okay in some situations for a person to take nude or sexual images of a partner without their permission
32. A person who shows their friends a nude or sexual image of another person without their permission shouldn't be punished if they did not mean to hurt the person
33. If you're in a consensual sexual relationship with someone, it's ok if they take nude or sexual images of you without your permission
34. If a woman is willing to send a nude or sexual image to someone she just met, then it's no big deal if they show it to their friends
35. Men tend to exaggerate the impact of having a nude or sexual image of themselves shared without their permission
36. If a person allows their partner to take a nude or sexual image of them, they should be okay with that image being shared with others

Note The 36 statements have been grouped according to the four components identified in Chapter 3. The non-assigned statements are included here for completeness but were excluded from subsequent statistical analyses

recent experience: funny, okay with it, not bothered by it, uncomfortable, annoyed, bad about it, sorry for the victim-survivor, angry at the perpetrator, and other (see Table 2.4). They were then asked whether they said or did anything in response to witnessing the incident. The nine feelings questions were measured via a five-point scale (ranging from 1 'not at all'

Table 2.3   Image-based sexual abuse behaviours

1. Someone creating/taking a nude or sexual image of another person without their permission
2. Someone sharing/showing others a nude or sexual image of another person without their permission
3. Someone threatening to share/show a nude or sexual image of another person
4. Someone sharing/uploading online a nude or sexual image of another person without their permission
5. Someone taking a photo or video up another person's skirt or shorts without their permission
6. Someone taking a photo or video of another person's cleavage without their permission
7. Any other behaviour you would classify as non-consensual imagery

to 5 'very much'), and the one response question was measured via two categorical response options ('no' and 'yes').

Perceptions of witnessing image-based sexual abuse: Participants were presented with one of eight versions of a scenario involving the non-consensual sharing of a sexual video (see Table 2.5). The scenarios differed according to the gender of the perpetrator (female perpetrator, male perpetrator), the gender of the victim-survivor (female victim-survivor, male victim-survivor), and the victim-survivor's initial consent to the sexual video (secretly recorded, self-recorded).

Perpetrator gender and victim-survivor gender were manipulated via the use of gendered nouns (i.e. boyfriend, girlfriend) and pronouns (i.e. his, him, himself, her, herself). Initial victim-survivor consent was manipulated via reference to the victim-survivor recording themselves performing

Table 2.4   Feelings about witnessing image-based sexual abuse

1. I thought it was funny
2. I was okay with it
3. It didn't bother me
4. I felt uncomfortable
5. I felt annoyed
6. I felt bad about it
7. I felt sorry for the person depicted in the image
8. I felt anger towards the person who did this
9. Other

Table 2.5 Example scenarios

Female perpetrator, male victim-survivor, self-recorded
Taylor has recently broken up with her boyfriend Sam, who is a good friend of yours. It was a nasty breakup with both sides posting rude comments about each other on Facebook and Instagram. When they were together, Sam sent Taylor a video of himself performing oral sex on her. Sometime after the breakup, Taylor sends the video to Sam's new girlfriend in order to embarrass him.

Male perpetrator, female victim-survivor, secretly recorded
Taylor has recently broken up with his girlfriend Sam, who is a good friend of yours. It was a nasty breakup with both sides posting rude comments about each other on Facebook and Instagram. When they were together, Taylor secretly recorded Sam performing oral sex on him. Sometime after the breakup, Taylor sends the video to Sam's new boyfriend in order to embarrass her.

---

a sexual act on the perpetrator, or the perpetrator secretly recording the victim-survivor performing a sexual act on them.

Having read the scenario, participants were asked about their 'behavioural intentions', and whether they would say or do anything if the victim-survivor told them what had happened. This question was measured via a five-point scale (ranging from 1 'definitely not' to 5 'definitely'). Participants were then asked an open-question regarding what they would say or do. Finally, participants were asked three 'what if' questions to determine whether their view of the situation would change if: (1) the gender of the perpetrator had been different; (2) the gender of the victim-survivor had been different; and (3) the victim-survivor's initial consent to the sexual video had been different. To illustrate, participants presented with the 'female perpetrator, male victim-survivor, self-recorded scenario' were asked whether their view of the situation would change if the perpetrator was a man, the victim-survivor was a woman, and the perpetrator had secretly recorded the victim-survivor performing a sexual act. Conversely, participants presented with the 'male perpetrator, female victim-survivor, secretly recorded' scenario were asked whether their view of the situation would change if the perpetrator was a woman, the victim-survivor was a man, and the victim-survivor had recorded themselves performing a sexual act. These questions were measured via a five-point scale (ranging from 1 'definitely not' to 5 'definitely') and were followed by open-questions regarding why their views would or would not change.

Beliefs regarding image-based sexual abuse laws: Participants were asked whether four forms of image-based sexual abuse (take, share,

Table 2.6   Forms of image-based sexual abuse

---

1. Create/take a nude or sexual image (photo or video) of someone without their permission.
2. Share/show a nude or sexual image (photo or video) of a someone without their permission.
3. Upload onto a website a nude or sexual image (photo or video) of someone without their permission.
4. Threaten to share a nude or sexual image (photo or video) of someone.

---

upload, and threaten to share) were currently a crime where they live, and whether they thought these behaviours should be a crime (see Table 2.6). The four questions regarding whether image-based sexual abuse is currently a crime were measured via three categorical response options ('no', 'unsure', and 'yes'). The four questions regarding whether image-based sexual abuse should be a crime were measured via five-point scales (ranging from 1 'definitely not' to 5 'definitely'). Importantly, all participants resided in states where image-based sexual abuse laws were in place at the time of the survey.

Demographic characteristics: Participants were asked to provide some basic demographic information, including their age, gender identity, sexuality, ethnicity, languages other than English spoken at home, level of education, employment status, and state of residence.

Analysis Approach

Statistical analysis was conducted using Jamovi, a free and open statistical platform. Descriptive analyses were performed to examine participants' attitudes towards intimate image sharing, experiences of witnessing image-based sexual abuse (including their most recent experience, where appropriate), perceptions of witnessing image-based sexual abuse, and beliefs regarding image-based sexual abuse laws. Principal components analysis was performed to explore the underlying structure of participants' attitudes towards intimate image sharing. Four components that grouped together were identified, which we labelled as 'blame', 'acceptable exceptions', 'positive impact', and 'minimisation'. Items that were not assigned to one of the four components were excluded from subsequent statistical analyses. T-test analyses were then performed to explore whether there was any gender- and sexuality-based differences in participants' attitudes towards image-based sexual abuse.

Analyses of variance were also performed to explore the influence of perpetrator gender, victim-survivor gender, and initial victim-survivor consent on perceptions of witnessing image-based sexual abuse, specifically, participants' behavioural intentions and responses to three what if questions. Thematic analyses were then conducted for the associated open-questions to develop and summarise key themes related to the witnessing of image-based sexual abuse. When reporting on these data, participants have been assigned a pseudonym based on their assigned survey number (e.g. P100), city of residence (e.g. ADE for Adelaide, SYD for Sydney), and gender (e.g. NB for non-binary). Finally, chi-square and t-test analyses were performed to explore whether there was any gender- and sexuality-based differences in participants' beliefs regarding image-based sexual abuse laws.

Unfortunately, it was not possible to include non-binary, transgender, or other gender identity participants in the statistical analyses due to the small numbers of participants who self-identified as such. This is a limitation of the study, discussed in more detail in Chapter 6. Given the exploratory nature of the current research, both significant and non-significant but noteworthy gender and sexuality differences are reported. Significant differences have an alpha value of $p < 0.05$, and non-significant (or partially significant) but noteworthy differences have an alpha value of $p \leq 0.10$.

Focus Groups

Sample/Setting

In May and June 2019, 35 focus groups were conducted in the capital cities of four Australian jurisdictions: Adelaide (South Australia), Canberra (Australian Capital Territory), Melbourne (Victoria), and Sydney (New South Wales). The focus group sample comprised 219 Australian adults. The variation in this number from the 245 participants who completed the survey was due to some participants completing the survey and then being unable to attend the requisite focus group, due to illness or another reason (see Table 2.7 for the number of focus groups and participants by location).

Table 2.7 Number of focus groups and participants by location

Location	Number of focus groups	Number of participants
Adelaide	10	60
Canberra	5	30
Melbourne	10	64
Sydney	10	65
Total	35	219

The focus groups were run by two facilitators. This ensured that if any participants became distressed or had an issue that required attention (e.g. running late), a second facilitator could attend to that person, rather than the focus group needing to pause or stop entirely. Two pilot focus groups were conducted in Melbourne with three facilitators so that one facilitator could observe and make any necessary changes to questions, approach, and structure. All focus groups were conducted face-to-face in a central location within the four capital cities.

The focus groups had an average duration of 60 minutes, with no more than eight participants in each group. Participants were provided with snacks, coffee, tea, and water, and were reimbursed for their time with a small monetary gift card.

Procedure/Materials

When participants arrived at the focus group location, they were provided with a copy of the explanatory statement to read and were asked to sign a consent form. They also filled in a separate sheet with their unique identifier to confirm they had completed the survey. Once all forms were collected, the facilitator advised participants on issues relating to how focus groups operate, some comments on confidentiality, respectful interactions, and what to do if anyone began to feel uncomfortable or distressed.

Each focus group included a discussion of two scenarios outlining different examples of image-based sexual abuse and questions pertaining to bystander information and resources. There were two versions of each scenario (see Table 2.8 or Appendix Table A.1 for details of the scenarios). The variation in the scenarios involved changes to the gender identity of the perpetrator and/or victim-survivor. These were developed so that we

Table 2.8 Two versions of the focus group scenarios

Scenario 1 (S1)
Maryam (woman, aged 21) has been seeing your friend Kai (man, aged 25) for about a week. Without any prior discussion, Maryam sends Kai a photo of herself completely naked. The next day, Kai shows the photo to a group of his friends (including you) during a broad discussion about sex.
In the alternate version, Maryam (victim-survivor) was replaced with Arjun (man, aged 25) and Kai (perpetrator) was replaced with Sarah (woman, aged 21).
Scenario 2 (S2)
You are on a train sitting near a transwoman named Alex (who you don't know). She is wearing a t-shirt and a skirt and is 20 years old. A 30-year-old man named Lou (who you also don't know) is sitting opposite Alex. He tries to engage Alex in conversation, but it is clear she doesn't know him, so she ignores him. Later, you see Lou using his iPhone to secretly take a photo up Alex's skirt. Alex doesn't know Lou has done this.
In the alternate scenario, Lou's (perpetrator) gender is changed to a woman.

---

could explore whether participants' views differed according to the gender identity of the people discussed in the scenario.

The original S1 and S2 versions were completed by 18 focus groups, and the alternate S1 and S2 versions were completed by 17 focus groups. The victim-survivor in S2 was identified as a transwoman. We included a transwoman in the scenario to directly respond to a clear gap in the literature on image-based sexual abuse perpetrated against transgender people (see, e.g., Flynn & Henry, 2021; Powell et al., 2020b). The names of the perpetrator and victim-survivor were also varied in the two versions of S1 to suggest that some were from non-majority racial groups, thereby allowing for potential discussions around race, ethnicity, and religion. The inclusion of names from non-majority racial groups and a transwoman also provided the opportunity to explore some of the intersections of marginalisation that have emerged as relevant in studies of image-based sexual abuse prevalence to date (see, e.g., Henry et al., 2019a, 2019b, 2020; Powell et al., 2020a, 2020b).

After reflecting on the scenario, participants were asked four sets of questions divided into action questions, context/intent questions, responsibility questions, and gender questions (see Table 2.9).

The final stage in the focus group considered avenues of support, such as the ways in which information and resources around image-based sexual abuse could be improved and possible delivery modes. Participants were asked if they were aware of any avenues of support available to either perpetrators or victim-survivors of image-based sexual abuse. Not

Table 2.9 Types of focus group questions

Action questions
Participants were asked if, and if so what, they would say or do in the given situation. This included whether they would say anything to the perpetrator, victim-survivor, and/or anyone else, what would make them more likely to say or do something, and what would be the biggest barrier and the biggest facilitator to them saying or doing something.

Content/intent questions
For S1, participants were asked if the intent of the perpetrator and/or victim-survivor would affect whether they would say or do anything, and if their opinion would change if the perpetrator had asked for the image of the victim-survivor. For S2, participants were asked if they would feel differently about the situation if the perpetrator and victim-survivor knew one another, if they personally knew the victim-survivor, and if they personally knew the perpetrator.

Responsibility questions
Participants were asked if the behaviour depicted in the scenario should be a crime, what would be an appropriate punishment if it was a crime, and the extent to which the victim-survivor was responsible for what happened. For S1, participants were also asked if the victim-survivor had broken the law, and if it should be a crime to send unsolicited naked images. For S2, participants were asked if the perpetrator had broken the law, and if the victim-survivor should report the behaviour to the police or someone else.

Gender questions
Participants were asked if they would feel differently about anything relating to the situation if the perpetrator's and/or victim-survivor's (S1 only) gender was altered from man to woman or woman to man. For S2, participants were asked if they would feel differently about anything relating to the situation if the perpetrator's gender was altered from man to woman or woman to man.

---

all questions were asked or asked in this specific order, depending on time restraints and the natural direction of discussions.

Participants were provided with a list of support services on the explanatory statement they received by email. They were also encouraged to email the project address if they had any questions. Additionally, the consent forms included an option for participants to receive a 'follow-up' email from the research team in the week after the focus group. If this option was selected, an email was sent to them the week after the focus group to check in on their well-being and any follow-up queries were responded to. Approximately 180 of the 219 participants requested a follow-up email. No negative responses or concerns were raised with the research team during the follow-ups.

Analysis Approach

With participants' permission, the focus groups were audio-recorded and transcribed verbatim by an external transcription company. The transcripts were checked for accuracy, and all identifying information about participants was removed. Participants were assigned a pseudonym based on the focus group number (e.g. FG1 for focus group 1) and location attended (e.g. ADE for Adelaide, SYD for Sydney), their gender (e.g. F for female), and participant number (e.g. 1). For example, male participant one in the third focus group in Adelaide would be referred to as FG3 ADE M1, and the fourth female participant in the third focus group in Sydney would be referred to as FG3 SYD F4. The transcripts were imported in NVivo version 12 (qualitative data analysis software) and thematically analysed. Six parent codes were developed for the two scenarios, including: (1) bystander action; (2) intent; (3) legal responses; (4) victim-blaming and responsibility; (5) gender; and (6) culture.

CONCLUSION

This chapter has provided an overview of the research questions, study methodology, and analysis process of the Image-Based Sexual Abuse and Bystander Intervention Study. The book now begins exploring the key research findings. In the next chapter, we start by examining participants' attitudes towards image-based sexual abuse.

REFERENCES

Cyber Civil Rights Initiative. (2014). *End revenge porn: A campaign of the Cyber Civil Rights Initiative*. Retrieved October 21, 2024, from https://www.cyb ercivilrights.org/wp-content/uploads/2014/12/RPStatistics.pdf

Englander, E. (2015). Coerced sexting and revenge porn among teens. *Bullying, Teen Aggression & Social Media, 1*(2), 19–21.

Flynn, A. (2023). Image-based sexual abuse. In H. Pontell (Ed.), *Oxford research encyclopedia of criminology and criminal justice* (2nd ed.). Oxford University Press. https://doi.org/10.1093/acrefore/9780190264079.013.534

Flynn, A., Cama, E., Powell, A., & Scott, A. J. (2023). Victim-blaming and image-based sexual abuse. *Journal of Criminology, 56*(1), 7–15. https://doi.org/10.1177/26338076221135327

Flynn, A., & Henry, N. (2021). Image-based sexual abuse: An Australian reflection. *Women and Criminal Justice, 31*(4), 313–326. https://doi.org/10.1080/08974454.2019.1646190

Henry, N., Flynn, A., & Powell, A. (2019a). *Responding to revenge pornography: The scope, nature and impact of Australian criminal laws—A report to the Criminology Research Council*. Australian Institute of Criminology. Retrieved October 21, 2024, from https://www.aic.gov.au/sites/default/files/2020-05/CRG_08_15-16-FinalReport.pdf

Henry, N., Flynn, A., & Powell, A. (2019). Image-based sexual abuse: Victims and perpetrators. *Trends & Issues in Crime and Criminal Justice, 572*, 1–19. https://doi.org/10.52922/ti09975

Henry, N., McGlynn, C., Flynn, A., Johnson, K., Powell, A., & Scott, A. J. (2020). *Image-based sexual abuse: A study on the causes and consequences of non-consensual nude or sexual imagery*. Routledge.

McAfee. (2013). *Love, relationships, and technology survey*. Retrieved October 21, 2024, from http://www.mcafee.com/us/about/news/2013/q1/20130204-01.aspx

Powell, A., Henry, N., Flynn, A., & Scott, A. J. (2019). Image-based sexual abuse: The extent, nature, and predictors of perpetration in a community sample of Australian adults. *Computers in Human Behavior, 92*, 393–402. https://doi.org/10.1016/j.chb.2018.11.009

Powell, A., Scott, A. J., Flynn, A., & Henry, N. (2020). *Image-based sexual abuse: An international study of victims and perpetrators*. RMIT University. Retrieved October 21, 2024, from https://www.researchgate.net/publication/339488012_Image-based_sexual_abuse_An_international_study_of_victims_and_perpetrators

Powell, A., Scott, A. J., Flynn, A., & McCook, S. (2022a). A multi-country study of image-based sexual abuse: Extent, relational nature and correlates of victimisation experiences. *Journal of Sexual Aggression, 30*(1), 25–40. https://doi.org/10.1080/13552600.2022.2119292

Powell, A., Scott, A. J., Flynn, A., & McCook, S. (2022b). Perpetration of image-based sexual abuse: Extent, nature and correlates in a multi-country sample. *Journal of Interpersonal Violence, 37*(23–24), 22864–22889. https://doi.org/10.1177/08862605211072266

Powell, A., Scott, A. J., & Henry, N. (2020b). Digital harassment and abuse: Experiences of sexuality and gender minority adults. *European Journal of Criminology, 17*(2), 199–223. https://doi.org/10.1177/1477370818788006

CHAPTER 3

Attitudes Towards Image-Based Sexual Abuse

Abstract This chapter explores Australians' attitudes towards image-based sexual abuse and how these attitudes may then shape or impact bystanders' intentions, readiness, and capacity to intervene when witnessing image-based sexual abuse behaviours. In doing so, we explore differences in survey participants' attitudes, with a specific focus on gender and sexuality. This chapter also focuses on the concept of victim-blaming, including how focus group participants assigned blame and responsibility to aspects of the victim-survivors' behaviour and actions. We unpack nuances of the scenarios presented to participants, including how varying the victim-survivor and perpetrator gender in the scenarios presented to participants played a role in influencing how they attributed blame and harm.

Keywords Image-based sexual abuse · Bystander · Intervention · Attitudes · Victim-blaming · Gender

© The Author(s), under exclusive license to Springer Nature
Switzerland AG 2025
A. Flynn et al., *Image-Based Sexual Abuse and Bystander Intervention*,
Palgrave Studies in Cybercrime and Cybersecurity,
https://doi.org/10.1007/978-3-031-83647-3_3

49

INTRODUCTION

There is extensive evidence that people hold attitudes of blame towards victim-survivors of sexual violence according to a range of factors, such as what the victim-survivor was wearing, whether they consumed alcohol or other drugs, and their relationship with the perpetrator (Burgin & Flynn, 2021; Pinciotti & Orcutt, 2021). Attitudes of blame have been linked to acceptance of myths surrounding sexual violence, as well as agreement with traditional gender roles (Grubb & Turner, 2012). Such attitudes of blame not only increase the harms of sexual violence, but can impact the likelihood of victim-survivors seeking help (Anderson & Overby, 2021; Flynn, 2015; Henry et al., 2015; Lichty & Gowen, 2021; Pijlman et al., 2024; Trottier et al., 2021). Research further suggests that when attitudes of blame are held by the police and those whom a victim may first disclose to (e.g. support workers, family, friends), they can negatively shape the responses provided (Mourtgos et al., 2021; O'Neal, 2019). This can lead to self-shaming and poor mental health outcomes for victim-survivors, as well as contributing to reduced social understandings of sexual violence.

In recent years, researchers have sought to understand whether attitudes towards sexual violence and victim-survivors extend to image-based sexual abuse (see Amudhan et al., 2024 for review). This body of research suggests that overall, men are more likely than women to blame victim-survivors of image-based sexual abuse, to have less empathy for victim-survivors, and to minimise the harms of image-based sexual abuse (Attrill-Smith et al., 2021; Bothamley & Tully, 2018; Flynn et al., 2023; Henry et al., 2019; Scott & Gavin, 2018; Zvi & Shechory Bitton, 2021). In an Australian survey of over 4,000 participants, Henry et al. (2019) found that 49% of male participants, compared with 32% of female participants, held attitudes that either minimised image-based sexual abuse harms, blamed victim-survivors, or excused perpetrators. In a cross-jurisdictional study on image-based sexual abuse across Australia, New Zealand, and the United Kingdom, Flynn et al. (2023) found that attitudes of blame and harm minimisation among participants were low. However, men were more likely than women to report that image-based sexual abuse could have positive impacts on victim-survivors and that there are some circumstances in which image-based sexual abuse is acceptable (Flynn et al., 2023). Other research has found that men are less likely to perceive the situation as serious or to see police intervention as necessary, and may perceive the perpetrator as deserving of a more lenient punishment compared to women (Bothamley & Tully, 2018; Fido et al., 2021; Scott & Gavin, 2018). There is also some evidence to suggest that men may perceive the situation to be more serious when it involves a male perpetrator and female victim-survivor, rather than a female perpetrator and male victim-survivor (Flynn et al., 2024a; Scott & Gavin, 2018), although other studies have not found these differences (Attrill-Smith et al., 2021; Sciacca et al., 2021). Research suggests that women's perceptions may not differ according to the gender of the perpetrator or victim-survivor (Scott & Gavin, 2018).

Researchers have found that people blame victim-survivors of image-based sexual abuse more where the relationship between the perpetrator and victim-survivor was of shorter duration, where there is greater nudity involved (e.g. breasts are exposed in images), and where the images were self-taken by the victim-survivor and later non-consensually shared by the perpetrator (Crawford & Popp, 2003; McKinlay & Lavis, 2020; Pina et al., 2021; Starr & Lavis, 2018; Zvi & Shechory Bitton, 2021). People who are more likely to accept sexual double standards, whereby they believe that women should be judged more harshly than men for the same sexual behaviours, also tend to attribute greater blame to victim-survivors of image-based sexual abuse (Aborisade, 2022; Mckinlay & Lavis, 2020; Ricciardelli & Adorjan, 2019). In focus groups with 115 teens aged 13 to 19 years, Ricciardelli and Adorjan (2019) found participants perpetuated these standards, with young women who sent sexual images labelled as 'sluts', compared to young men who sent images having their actions described as 'typical behaviour'. Lippman and Campbell (2014) similarly found girls were judged harshly when they shared images (labelled as 'sluts') and when they did not (labelled as 'prudes'), while boys received no such judgement. Ringrose et al. (2013) also found that while young people may perceive sexting as a normal part of sexual development, there were still more negative judgements towards young women who engaged in this behaviour. There is some evidence that personal experience in sending sexual images may influence attitudes towards image-based sexual abuse. For instance, research has found that people without experience sending sexual self-images may be more likely to hold the victim-survivor responsible, be more likely to believe the situation is serious, and be less likely to minimise the harms than those with experience of sending sexual self-images (Flynn et al., 2023; Scott & Gavin, 2018).

The literature suggests there is a need to further examine attitudes that may contribute to victim-blaming and the minimisation of image-based sexual abuse harms. This is especially important given research conducted with image-based sexual abuse victim-survivors suggests they experience feelings of blame when first disclosing, which can act as a barrier to reporting and/or help seeking (Bates, 2017; Henry et al., 2020; McGlynn et al., 2021). Research has found that victim-survivors of image-based sexual abuse are less likely to seek help compared to victim-survivors of contact-based sexual violence (Pijlman & Boertien, 2024). In a recent review of help-seeking behaviour, researchers found that one of the most frequently identified factors affecting help seeking was fear of the negative social responses of telling others, with some studies specifically reporting actual responses from others of victim-blaming, of not being taken seriously, or of being judged and misunderstood (Pijlman et al., 2024).

In this chapter, we explore participants' attitudes towards image-based sexual abuse in the Image-Based Abuse and Bystander Intervention Study, including the gendered differences in attitudes. This chapter also focuses on the concept of victim-blaming, including how participants assigned blame and responsibility to aspects of the victim-survivors' behaviour and actions in the hypothetical scenarios presented. We unpack nuances of the scenarios presented to participants, including how varying the victim-survivor and perpetrator gender in the scenarios played a role in influencing how participants attributed blame and harm.

ATTITUDES TOWARDS IMAGE-BASED SEXUAL ABUSE

In the Image-Based Sexual Abuse and Bystander Intervention Study, we sought to understand attitudes of blame and minimisation of harms held by Australian adults. Survey participants indicated their level of agreement with 36 statements relating to attitudes towards image-based sexual abuse, specifically around the sharing of intimate (nude or sexual) imagery (see Table 2.2 in Chapter 2). Principal components analysis was then performed and identified four components that grouped together: (1) blame; (2) acceptable exceptions; (3) positive impact; and (4) minimisation. The blame component comprises 11 statements reflecting the view that people should not take or share intimate images of themselves if they do not want these images to be shared. For example, people are partly to blame if they share nude or sexual images of themselves and should not expect their images to remain private. The acceptable exceptions component comprises three statements reflecting the view that it is acceptable to share intimate images in certain situations. For example, it is okay to share nude or sexual images if a person did not want or ask for them (e.g. if they received an unsolicited 'dick pic'), or if the images were sent by someone they did not know well. The positive impact component comprises seven statements reflecting the view that people may benefit from intimate image sharing. For example, people can boost their reputation by sharing nude or sexual images and find it a turn-on to have their images shared. The minimisation component comprises nine statements reflecting the view that intimate image sharing is of little consequence. For example, people tend to exaggerate the impact of having a nude or sexual image shared and should not get upset. The six remaining statements were not assigned to one of these components because they had similar or low loadings on more than one component, and were excluded from subsequent statistical analyses.

Overall, participants expressed the greatest level of agreement with the blame statements (M = 2.61) and the least level of agreement with the minimisation component (M = 1.36; see Table 3.1). Encouragingly, participants generally demonstrated a low level of agreement across all four components, with no average score exceeding the midpoint of the scales (4 'neither disagree nor agree'). This suggests that most participants did not agree with statements of blame, acceptable exceptions, positive impacts, or minimisation of harms.

Table 3.1 Attitudes towards intimate image sharing, M (SD)

	Overall (n = 245)	Gender		Sexuality	
		Female (n = 161)	Male (n = 73)	LGBQI+ (n = 62)	Hetero (n = 183)
Blame	2.61 (1.55)	2.44 (1.47)	3.09 (1.66)	2.31 (1.35)	2.71 (1.61)
Acceptable exceptions	2.53 (1.45)	2.35 (1.33)	2.85 (1.62)	2.96 (1.53)	2.38 (1.39)
Positive impact	2.05 (0.93)	1.97 (0.83)	2.26 (1.11)	2.12 (0.91)	2.03 (0.94)
Minimisation	1.36 (0.58)	1.25 (0.42)	1.64 (0.80)	1.37 (0.70)	1.35 (0.54)

Note Measured via a 7-point scale ranging from 1 'strongly disagree' to 7 'strongly agree'. Gender comparisons utilise a slightly smaller sample ($n = 234$) because there were insufficient non-binary, transgender, or other gender identity participants ($n = 11$) for statistical analyses

Given the extensive literature suggesting that men attribute higher blame to victim-survivors of sexual violence more broadly, and of image-based sexual violence specifically, we sought to test differences according to gender in this study. There is very limited research on how such attitudes towards image-based sexual abuse vary according to sexuality, with some evidence to suggest that heterosexual people are more likely to blame victim-survivors (Flynn et al., 2023), so we also sought to explore these differences in our research. Regarding gender comparisons, male participants reported significantly higher levels of agreement with statements across all four components compared to female participants: M = 3.09 vs. M = 2.44 for blame; M = 2.85 vs. M = 2.35 for acceptable exceptions; M = 2.26 vs. M = 1.97 for positive impact; and M = 1.64 vs. M = 1.25 for minimisation. Regarding sexuality comparisons, LGBQI+ participants reported a significantly higher level of agreement with the acceptable exceptions statements (M = 2.96 vs. M = 2.38), and a lower level of agreement with the blame statements (M = 2.31 vs. M = 2.71) compared to heterosexual participants. There were no significant differences in agreement with the positive impacts or minimisation statements according to sexuality.

Collectively, these findings suggest that men and heterosexual individuals are more likely to blame victim-survivors of image-based sexual abuse if they have previously taken or shared intimate images of themselves, and men are more likely to believe that intimate image sharing is acceptable in certain situations (e.g. when the images were not wanted or asked for). Similar findings were evident in a survey of over 6,000 adults across Australia, New Zealand, and the United Kingdom, which found that men, heterosexual participants, and those who had perpetrated more image-based sexual abuse behaviours tended to attribute more blame to victim-survivors of image-based sexual abuse, and to minimise the harms of this form of violence to a greater extent (Flynn et al., 2023).

The higher levels of blame and minimisation of harms among men, and of blame among heterosexual individuals, may be due to the gendered and heteronormative dynamics that shape risk, blame, and responsibility in sexual image sharing (Flynn et al., 2023). Another potential explanation for this difference in attitudes based on sexual orientation may be because LGBQI+ people are more likely to engage in consensual image sharing behaviours (Comunello et al., 2021; Flynn et al., 2024b; Van Ouytsel et al., 2020a, 2020b), and to use dating apps online (Flynn et al., 2024b; Johnson et al., 2017), where images are commonly shared, which may reduce some of the stigma around intimate image sharing (Paradiso et al., 2024).

Our survey findings also suggest that men are more likely to believe people can boost their reputation by sharing intimate images and that people feel turned-on by having their images shared. Connections between this finding and gendered views emerging in the focus groups are discussed in more detail in a later section and in Chapter 5. Finally, the findings suggest that men are more likely to minimise the impacts of image-based sexual abuse and believe that victim-survivors should not get upset because of having their images shared. These findings support previous research. For example, in a study of over 4,000 Australians aged 16 to 49 years, Henry et al. (2019) found that 70% of participants agreed that 'people should know better than to take nude selfies in the first place, even if they never send them to anyone', while 62% agreed that 'if a person sends a nude or sexual image to someone else, then they are at least partly responsible if the image ends up online'. Overall, 67% of men and 57% of women held these views (Henry et al., 2019). Similar victim-blaming attitudes can be seen in public commentary on image-based sexual abuse, whereby there is a clear 'normalising [of] men's sexual entitlement to women's bodies, whilst shaming and denying sexual subjectivity to women victim-survivors' (Henry et al., 2020, p. 131).

VICTIM-BLAMING AND BYSTANDERS

To further explore attitudes of blame in the context of bystander inter-vention, we asked focus group participants to what extent they perceived that the victim-survivors in both scenarios (S1 and S2) were respon-sible for the actions of the perpetrators (see Table 2.8 in Chapter 2 or Appendix Table A.1 for details of the scenarios). In response to S1, there were mixed views emerging on blame. Some participants described the victim-survivor as having some blame or responsibility for their intimate image being shared because they had sent the image of themselves to the other person in the first place. Previous research has found similar attitudes of blame towards victim-survivors who took the image them-selves, which was later non-consensually shared (McKinlay & Lavis, 2020; Zvi & Shechory Bitton, 2021). In the current study, perceptions of blame ranged from participants identifying the victim-survivor as being highly responsible: 'I'd say 80% responsible for the image being shared' (FG1 ADE F2), to being partially responsible: 'you must know a little bit that if you send this image there could be consequences and this could be one of them. So yeah, there might be some partial blame' (FG8 ADE F1). Some participants also made explicit statements blaming the victim-survivor:

> Wake up to yourself, lass. This is going out into that cyberspace. You're not doing yourself any favours. (FG4 CAN F2)

> If you send a photo like that to anyone, you're expecting it to be either shown to your mates or online. ... You expect it to be shared with someone. (FG5 MEL F4)

This view became more prevalent when participants reflected on the unsolicited nature of the image, where there was a common view that this alleviated some of the responsibility from the person showing the image to their friendship group, because there was no consent in the initial sending or receiving of the image. As these comments demonstrate:

> He put the picture out there in the first place without being asked. He willingly sent the photo. (FG4 MEL F3)

> I wish that people were not as dumb as they appear to be. So, I wish that people did not send unsolicited photographs of themselves naked. (FG3 ADE F1)

> If both people have acted without consent, it kind of cancels out. (FG5 SYD F2).

A similar view was expressed by the following participants in one of the focus groups (FG2 CAN):

> F1: If he sends an unsolicited image, he's basically lost control of it and it's up to her what she wants to do with it. If she wants to show it to friends, that's fine as far as I'm concerned.

> M1: If he sent it to her unsolicited, he's lost control of it. It's not up to him to say what happens.

Factors such as how long and how well the victim-survivor had known the person before sending them the intimate image—the perceived nature of their relationship—were also identified as increasing their responsibility for it being shared among others. In this scenario, participants believed the victim-survivor was more responsible because they had only known the perpetrator for a short period of time. This finding is similar to previous research, which has found that higher levels of blame are attributed where the relationship was of shorter duration (Starr & Lavis, 2018). As the following participants in the current study observed:

> What was she thinking? Who sends someone a photo of themselves naked, like having literally known each other for a week? (FG10 ADE F2)

> People really shouldn't be sending texts of themselves naked after only knowing someone a week. And you're really opening yourself up to ridicule if you do that for someone you've only known for a very short time. (FG8 MEL M1)

> If you only have known him for a week, you probably don't know everything about him. You never know what's going to happen, especially with, like, something so sensitive about your body. ... You should expect that coming, that's what I think. (FG7 SYD F3)

In the discussions of S1, references to the victim-survivor engaging in risky behaviour were also common among participants, with many using the terms 'risk' or 'risky' when describing the actions of the victim-survivor in sending the image initially. These terms were often then accompanied by statements of blame or responsibilisation on the victim-survivor for the perpetrator's actions:

> He's engaging in risky behaviours in the first place. If he is not happy for that image to be public consumption, then he shouldn't be sending it to anybody, because there is a risk that that image is not going to be kept by that person for their eyes only. (FG3 CAN F3)

> It's just being aware of the risk when you choose to make the decision to send the photo. She just needs to be aware that it [the perpetrator sharing the image] is a possible outcome. (FG1 MEL M2)

> When you send out a photo like that, you need to be cautious, and you need to think of the risks associated with it landing in the wrong hands. So, I think to an extent, she does have a bit of responsibility. (FG8 MEL F3)

While in some instances, participants shied away from using the terms 'blame' or 'responsibility', participants instead described the behaviour as being 'risky'. These statements still indicate that these participants perceived the victim-survivor as having taken some action that created the possibility of victimisation occurring:

> You're opening yourself up to risk. So, you're responsible for opening yourself up to that risk. (FG1 CAN F1)

> I'm quite uncomfortable with calling or using the word responsible for her. I think what she did is very risky, but I wouldn't go as far as to say she's responsible for what he did with it, because that was still his choice, and he could've shared it or deleted it or done whatever he wanted with it. (FG7 SYD F4)

This view was summarised by one participant as the victim-survivor 'becoming the victim of what she's actually done' (FG8 SYD F1).

Some participants expressed a view that both the victim-survivor and the perpetrator had a shared level of responsibility and blame for their respective actions:

> I think the responsibility should go to Arjun [victim-survivor] and Sarah [perpetrator] equally because both have the responsibility – because Arjun is the person who shared it first, then Sarah shared it next. So, I think both bears the responsibility. (FG3 MEL F2)

> He's made a dumb decision, so he was the cause of it, but the moral reprehensibility is placed solely on Sarah [perpetrator] in that regard. However, he can't be disregarded when it comes to the blame. But he's not the whole blame, because while he gave her the content, she was the one who allowed the content to be spread around, which is the actual reprehensible act. (FG2 CAN F2)

Some participants quite strongly advocated that no blame should be placed on the victim-survivor, arguing that all responsibility lay with the perpetrator for sharing the image with their friendship group. As one participant stated, 'It's completely on the person that shares it, not on the sender' (FG7 MEL F1). Similar views were expressed in another focus group (FG3 SYD), where Sarah had been described as sharing the image with others:

F1: He's [the victim-survivor] not at all responsible.

F2: In terms of sharing, I don't think he is responsible for Sarah's actions.

M1: Yeah, because she's broken boundaries – massive boundaries. So, whatever happens to her is on her from that point forward.

Other participants reflected on the policing of people's bodies as problematic, reflecting much of the narrative in existing research on consensual image sharing (Albury & Crawford, 2012; Burn, 2009; Crofts et al., 2015; Flynn & Henry, 2021; Henry et al., 2018, 2020; McGlynn & Rackley, 2017; Powell et al., 2019). As one participant stated, 'It's her body, her image, she owns it. She chose to share it with him, no-one else' (FG8 ADE M1).

While the 'murky' nature of consent contributed to some participants blaming the victim-survivor in S1, the more obvious absence of consent in S2 contributed to almost all participants attributing no blame to the victim-survivor. Indeed, when the same question around responsibility or blame was asked in relation to S2, all participants agreed that the victim-survivor (Alex) had 'zero' responsibility for her victimisation. In one focus group (FG1 MEL), the difference in the degree of victim-blaming between the two scenarios was observed by participants, albeit framed around how it would impact the victim-survivor, as opposed to the responsibility they placed on them:

M1: The difference is this one [S2] was non-consensual, where the other one [S1], he chose to send it.

M2: Some of these, when you take the photos for yourself, but if you share it with someone else, then yeah, it's a different thing. Because there's already a developed relationship.

F1: Yeah, I get what you mean. This is someone on a train taking a picture up your skirt, it's not like you took it and gave it to them.

F2: You're on a train, you're supposed to be going from one place to another, not having this sort of shit. The other one [S1] was people who knew each other had sent a photo. I just find this one is a lot more problematic.

M1: This one [S2] can be more mentally traumatic.

While there was firm agreement that Alex [victim-survivor] was not to blame in S2, some participants suggested that they would encourage Alex to be mindful about her state of dress in public:

> I'd probably make her aware that it was possible to take a photo up her skirt. Like, if he [the perpetrator] can do it, then anyone else can do it. I'd say, 'Maybe sit with your legs crossed'. (FG2 ADE F1)

> I'd probably tell Alex to fix her skirt. (FG6 MEL F4)

In another focus group, a participant reflected on their experiences observing women on public transport and noted they would likely take a similar approach with the victim-survivor in this situation:

> In the summertime, I've actually said to a couple of girls, ... 'You need to be aware that men are standing near you for a reason, because they're ...', I mean, it's summer. It's hot. A button has come undone, and I've chosen probably to embarrass them, more because I think they need to know that they need to cover up a little bit. (FG10 MEL M2)

These attitudes are an extension of the narrative used to frame women in other forms of sexual violence, such as sexual assault, harassment and rape, and are highly problematic (Flynn, 2015; Henry et al., 2020). Such narratives rely on blaming and shaming, women in particular, for putting themselves in risky environments (Flynn, 2015). In a more positive vein, there were very few comments like this across the focus groups, but this finding highlights the importance of education and messaging that challenges problematic attitudes and victim-blaming cultures that can legitimise or excuse abusive treatment of others and prevent victim-survivors from seeking assistance. In the context of bystander intervention, challenging victim-blaming attitudes is particularly important to ensure that the reactions of other bystanders do not normalise or support abusive behaviour and thereby dissuade intervention, or be seen as supporting the abusive behaviour, leading to a lack of action (Voelpel et al., 2008). We explore such barriers and facilitators to bystander intervention in more detail in Chapter 4.

Discussions of Gender

As discussed in relation to the survey responses, male participants were more likely to believe that the sharing of intimate images was a way that someone can boost their reputation. Gendered perceptions of the people in the hypothetical scenario also played into the attitudes participants held towards the person, including perceptions of the perpetrator's motivations and the harms experienced by the victim-survivor from the image-based sexual abuse incident. This was particularly evident in S1, and the perceived differing motivations informing the perpetrator's decision to non-consensually show an intimate image to their group of friends.

Research by Ringrose and colleagues (2012) suggests that sharing images without consent may form part of male bonding and a way to establish status among their peers. In our research, overwhelmingly, when the perpetrator was a man in S1, participants felt that the motivation was to sexualise the victim-survivor, to boost the perpetrator's standing among his peers, and to 'brag' about his dating conquest:

> If they're just having a general chitchat and then he's just whipped out his phone, 'Check this out fellas', … it's almost like he's showing off, oh look someone sent me a nude photo of themselves. So, it really speaks to his ego and his peer group. (FG10 ADE F2)

> In general, a man showing that is just because they love to have fun and showing off the girl in this photo like that, and look at this porn I got sent. That's normal for a guy. (FG9 SYD F5)

When the perpetrator was woman, the motivation was considered to be either to laugh at or humiliate the person who had sent the unsolicited image, or to indicate their distress at receiving the image. This suggests that participants assumed men would be less likely to experience distress from such an experience compared to women. This can be seen in the following comment reflective of those made across the focus groups:

> If a girl is doing that, it feels like she maybe – I don't know whether she's doing it under some distress. (FG9 SYD F5)

Similar findings emerge in the small number of studies that have explored attitudes towards image-based sexual abuse (Bothamley & Tully,

2018; Hudson et al., 2014; Pina et al., 2017; Scott & Gavin, 2018). In Scott and Gavin's (2018) study, for example, when presented with two hypothetical scenarios—one with a male perpetrator and female victim-survivor and one with a female perpetrator and male victim-survivor—participants perceived the scenario involving the male perpetrator and female victim-survivor to be more serious. This view was similarly evident in our focus groups with participants reflecting more negatively on the behaviour of the person for sending the image initially when the participant was a man, as opposed to a woman, assuming that the behaviour was somehow motivated by sexual gratification or 'creepiness'. In these instances, participants alleviated responsibility from the perpetrator and placed responsibility firmly onto the person who sent the image. As these participants observed:

> This man's sent a woman a naked picture of himself, which creepy men do all the time, and I think that changes the context where it's like, this is actually not just some consensual behaviour people are engaging in together. Like him actually just violating her by sending a picture to shock [her], and get off on how uncomfortable she is, because that's what guys on the internet and texting do a lot, well then that's different if she's sharing that around. I think it's a different issue of consent then, because then it's like he's actually the person who's aggressive and committing a violation by sending it. (FG3 CAN F1)

> They didn't discuss it. ... The fact is, he just sent the picture. ... He shouldn't have sent it in the first place, because that's very inappropriate. (FG3 CAN M2)

In contrast, when the person sharing the image was a woman, there was no suggestion that she was sexually violating the person who received the unsolicited image or that she was being creepy or inappropriate, but there were some gendered assumptions made, including that she may be vulnerable or sexually promiscuous:

> I'd make a judgment about her. I'd consider her a tramp and I'd probably say to the guy [perpetrator] that if you've shown it, she deserves it. (FG7 MEL M1)

> I think the woman probably, even if she sent it unsolicited herself, ... I think she probably is more vulnerable. (FG4 ADE F1)

I think she put herself in a vulnerable position. (FG4 CAN F1)

These views reflect the findings of Flynn et al.'s (2023) study involving interviews with stakeholders on image-based sexual abuse and victim-blaming, in which sexual double standards were found to inform attitudes, with participants noting women were pressured and expected to engage in sexting, but then blamed and punished for doing so. This is despite evidence that many people perceive sexting as a normative part of sexual development, and that women and girls may also be judged harshly when they do not share such images (Lippman & Campbell, 2014; Ringrose et al., 2013).

Several participants further reflected on the vulnerability of being a woman and receiving an unsolicited nude image as impacting on their attitude towards the incident. This view is reflected in the following comment:

> I see it more as maybe it's more of a bragging thing or something if a guy's sharing the image. I tend to see the woman as the more vulnerable person in that scenario. (FG4 CAN M1)

Across the focus groups, very few participants believed that a man would share a non-consensual image because they were distressed or seeking support, or that a woman would be bragging or sexualising the person in the image.

> I would be concerned for her. ... I would be like, this guy is coming onto you. ... I'd be more concerned for how she was feeling about it. (FG4 SYD F2)

This difference in view based on gender was similarly discussed in one of the focus groups (FG4 CAN):

> F1: I'd probably be more upset about Kai [perpetrator] sending it than the other way around. If Kai showed you that, you'd feel more strongly that what he did was wrong.

> M2: Yeah, I agree. I think it's society's stereotypical gender roles, it would make me put more blame on the male. ... I mean, I think what I'm saying in terms of just context here. ... Like we assume in this case with

Kai showing the picture that it's almost gloating or bragging. But if the reverse was true, it would be more disgust or shock.

While these views are highly representative of social gender norms, they contrast with research examining perpetrator motivations for engaging in image-based sexual abuse behaviours, which shows little difference according to gender. In their study of image-based sexual abuse perpetration across Australia, New Zealand, and the United Kingdom, of the 1,070 participants who reported engaging in the non-consensual taking, sharing, or threatening to share nude or sexual images, Henry et al. (2020) found no significant difference between male and female participants who identified their most common motivation being because it was 'fun' or 'sexy'. Similarly, despite participants in our study suggesting that men would be motivated by impressing their friendship group or sexualising the person in the image, and women would be motivated by distress, Henry et al. (2020) found no significant difference between female and male perpetrators with regard to 'wanting to impress friends' as their main motivation.

Conclusion

This chapter has explored participants' attitudes towards image-based sexual abuse, with a focus on gendered comparisons. It also explored victim-blaming, including how participants assigned blame and responsibility to victim-survivors in the hypothetical scenarios, and how varying the victim-survivor and perpetrator gender played a role in influencing how they attributed blame and harm. These findings have been discussed in the context of the literature available on victim-blaming in the context of image-based sexual abuse. In the next chapter, we explore how these attitudes may impact bystander intervention and identify key barriers and facilitators to bystander intervention in image-based sexual abuse incidents.

References

Aborisade, R. A. (2022). Image-based sexual abuse in a culturally conservative Nigerian society: Female victims' narratives of psychosocial costs. *Sexuality Research and Social Policy, 19*, 220–232. https://doi.org/10.1007/s13178-021-00536-3

Amudhan, S., Sharma, M. K., Anand, N., & Johnson, J. (2024). "Snapping, sharing and receiving blame": A systematic review on psychosocial factors of victim blaming in non-consensual pornography. *Industrial Psychiatry Journal, 33*(1), 3–12. https://doi.org/10.4103/ipj.ipj_166_23

Albury, K., & Crawford, K. (2012). Sexting, consent and young people's ethics: Beyond Megan's story. *Continuum Journal of Media & Cultural Studies, 26*(3), 463–473. https://doi.org/10.1080/10304312.2012.665840

Anderson, G. D., & Overby, R. (2021). The impact of rape myths and current events on the well-being of sexual violence survivors. *Violence against Women., 27*(9), 1379–1401. https://doi.org/10.1177/1077801220937782

Attrill-Smith, A., Wesson, C. J., Chater, M. L., & Weekes, L. (2021). Gender differences in videoed accounts of victim blaming for revenge porn for self-taken and stealth-taken sexually explicit images and videos. *Cyberpsychology: Journal of Psychosocial Research on Cyberspace, 15*(4), Article 3. https://doi.org/10.5817/CP2021-4-3

Bates, S. (2017). Revenge porn and mental health: A qualitative analysis of the mental health effects of revenge porn on female survivors. *Feminist Criminology, 12*(1), 22–42. https://doi.org/10.1177/1557085116654565

Bothamley, S., & Tully, R. J. (2018). Understanding revenge pornography: Public perceptions of revenge pornography and victim-blaming. *Journal of Aggression, Conflict and Peace Research, 10*(1), 1–10. https://doi.org/10.1108/JACPR-09-2016-0253

Burn, S. M. (2009). A situational model of sexual assault prevention through bystander intervention. *Sex Roles: A Journal of Research, 60*(11–12), 779–792. https://doi.org/10.1007/s11199-008-9581-5

Burgin, R., & Flynn, A. (2021). Women's behavior as implied consent: Male "reasonableness" in Australian rape law. *Criminology & Criminal Justice, 21*(3), 334–352. https://doi.org/10.1177/1748895819880953

Comunello, F., Parisi, L., & Ieracitano, F. (2021). Negotiating gender scripts in mobile dating apps: Between affordances, usage norms and practices. *Information, Communication & Society, 24*(8), 1140–1156. https://doi.org/10.1080/1369118X.2020.1787485

Crawford, M., & Popp, D. (2003). Sexual double standards: A review and methodological critique of two decades of research. *Journal of Sex Research, 40*(1), 13–26. https://doi.org/10.1080/00224490309552163

Crofts, T., Lee, M., McGovern, A., & Milivojevic, S. (2015). *Sexting and young people*. Palgrave Macmillan.

Fido, D., Harper, C. A., Davis, M. A., Petronzi, D., & Worrall, S. (2021). Intrasexual competition as a predictor of women's judgments of revenge pornography offending. *Sexual Abuse, 33*(3), 295–320. https://doi-org.www proxy1.library.unsw.edu.au/10.1177/1079063219894306

Flynn, A. (2015). Sexual violence and innovative responses to justice: Interrupting the recognisable narratives. In A. Powell, N. Henry, & A. Flynn (Eds.), *Rape justice: Beyond the criminal law* (pp. 92–111). Palgrave Macmillan.

Flynn, A., Cama, E., Powell, A., & Scott, A. J. (2023). Victim-blaming and image-based sexual abuse. *Journal of Criminology, 56*(1), 7–15. https://doi.org/10.1177/26338076221135327

Flynn, A., Scott, A. J., & Cama, E. (2024a). An empirical research study on barriers, facilitators, and strategies to promote bystander intervention in intimate image abuse contexts. In K. Summerer & G. M. Caletti (Eds.), *Criminalising intimate image abuse* (pp. 376–399). Oxford University Press.

Flynn, A., & Henry, N. (2021). Image-based sexual abuse: An Australian reflection. *Women and Criminal Justice, 31*(4), 313–326. https://doi.org/10.1080/08974454.2019.1646190

Flynn, A., Wheildon, L., Robards, B., Vakhitova, Z., & Harris, B. (2024b) *Australian users' experiences with control features on social media services and online dating apps: Key findings.* Retrieved October 21, 2024, from https://research.monash.edu/files/571453440/australian_users_experiences_with_control_features_on_social_media_services_and_online_dating_apps_final_report_may2023.pdf

Grubb, A., & Turner, E. (2012). Attribution of blame in rape cases: A review of the impact of rape myth acceptance, gender role conformity and substance use on victim blaming. *Aggression and Violent Behavior, 17*(5), 443–452. https://doi.org/10.1016/j.avb.2012.06.002

Henry, N., Flynn, A., & Powell, A. (2018). Policing image-based sexual abuse: Stakeholder perspectives. *Police Practice and Research: An International Journal, 19*(6), 565–581. https://doi.org/10.1080/15614263.2018.1507892

Henry, N., Flynn, A., & Powell, A. (2019). *Responding to revenge pornography: The scope, nature and impact of Australian criminal laws—A report to the Criminology Research Council.* Australian Institute of Criminology. Retrieved October 21, 2024, from https://www.aic.gov.au/sites/default/files/2020-05/CRG_08_15-16-FinalReport.pdf

Henry, N., McGlynn, C., Flynn, A., Johnson, K., Powell, A., & Scott, A. J. (2020). *Image-based sexual abuse: A study on the causes and consequences of non-consensual nude or sexual imagery.* Routledge.

Henry, N., Powell, A., & Flynn, A. (2015). The promise and paradox of justice: Rape justice beyond the criminal law. In A. Powell, N. Henry, & A. Flynn (Eds.), *Rape justice: Beyond the criminal law* (pp. 1–17). Palgrave Macmillan.

Hudson, H., Fetro, J., & Ogletree, R. (2014). Behavioral indicators and behaviors related to sexting among undergraduate students. *American Journal of Health Education, 45*(3), 183–195. https://doi.org/10.1080/19325037. 2014.901113

Johnson, K., Vilceanu, M. O., & Pontes, M. C. (2017). Use of online dating websites and dating apps: Findings and implications for LGB populations. *Journal of Marketing Development and Competitiveness, 11*(3). https://articl egateway.com/index.php/JMDC/article/view/1623

Lichty, L. F., & Gowen, L. K. (2021). Youth response to rape: Rape myths and social support. *Journal of Interpersonal Violence, 36*(11–12), 5530–5557. https://doi.org/10.1177/0886260518805777

Lippman, J. R., & Campbell, S. W. (2014). Damned if you do, damned if you don't…if you're a girl: Relational and normative contexts of adolescent sexting in the United States. *Journal of Children and Media, 8*(4), 371–386. https:// doi.org/10.1080/17482798.2014.923009

McGlynn, C., & Rackley, E. (2017). Image-based sexual abuse. *Oxford Journal of Legal Studies, 37*(3), 534–561. https://doi.org/10.1093/ojls/gqw033

McGlynn, C., Rackley, E., Johnson, K., Henry, N., Gavey, N., Flynn, A., & Powell, A. (2021). 'It's torture for the soul:' The harms of image-based sexual abuse. *Social & Legal Studies, 30*(4), 541–562. https://doi.org/10.1177/ 0964663920947791

Mckinlay, T., & Lavis, T. (2020). Why did she send it in the first place? Victim-blame in the context of 'revenge porn.' *Psychiatry, Psychology and Law, 27*(3), 386–396. https://doi.org/10.1080/13218719.2020.1734977

Mourtgos, S. M., Adams, I. T., & Mastracci, S. (2021). Improving victim engagement and officer response in rape investigations: A longitudinal assessment of a brief training. *Journal of Criminal Justice, 74*, 1–10. https://doi. org/10.1016/j.jcrimjus.2021.101818

O'Neal, E. N. (2019). 'Victim is not credible': The influence of rape culture on police perceptions of sexual assault complainants. *Justice Quarterly, 36*(1), 127–160. https://doi.org/10.1080/07418825.2017.1406977

Paradiso, M. N., Rollè, L., & Trombetta, T. (2024). Image-based sexual abuse associated factors: A systematic review. *Journal of Family Violence, 39*, 931–954. https://doi.org/10.1007/s10896-023-00557-z

Pijlman, V., & Boertien, E. (2024). A comparative study of the help-seeking behavior of victims of contact sexual violence and image-based sexual harassment and abuse. *Violence Against Women*. Advanced dation. https://doi.org/ 10.1177/10778012241283496

Pijlman, V., Waardt, M., Schoonmade, L., Eichelsheim, V., & Pemberton, A. (2024). The help-seeking behavior of victims of image-based sexual harassment and abuse: A scoping review. *Trauma, Violence & Abuse*. Advance online publication. https://doi.org/10.1177/15248380241289435

Pina, A., Bell, A., Griffin, K., & Vasquez, E. (2021). Image-based sexual abuse proclivity and victim-blaming: The role of dark personality traits and moral disengagement. *Oñati Socio-Legal Series, 11*(5), 1179–1197.

Pina, A., Holland, J., & James, M. (2017). The malevolent side of revenge porn proclivity: Dark personality traits and sexist ideology. *International Journal of Technoethics, 8*(1), 30–43. https://doi.org/10.4018/IJT.2017010103

Pinciotti, C. M., & Orcutt, H. K. (2021). Understanding gender differences in rape victim blaming: The power of social influence and just world beliefs. *Journal of Interpersonal Violence, 36*(1–2), 255–275. https://doi.org/10.1177/0886260517725736

Powell, A., Flynn, A., & Henry, N. (2019). Sexual violence in digital society: Human, technical and social factors. In T. Holt & R. Lukfeld (Eds.), *Understanding the human factor of cybercrime* (pp. 134–155). Routledge.

Ringrose, J., Gill, R., Livingstone, S., & Harvey, L. (2012). *A qualitative study of children, young people and 'sexting': A report prepared for the NSPCC.* Retrieved November 7, 2024, from https://eprints.lse.ac.uk/44216/1/__Libfile_repository_Content_Livingstone%2C%20S_A%20qualitative%20study%20of%20children%2C%20young%20people%20and%20%27sexting%27%20%28LSE%20RO%29.pdf

Sciacca, B., Mazzone, A., O'Higgins Norman, J., & Foody, M. (2021). Blame and responsibility in the context of youth produced sexual imagery: The role of teacher empathy and rape myth acceptance. *Teaching and Teacher Education, 103*, 1–9. https://doi.org/10.1016/j.tate.2021.103354

Scott, A. J., & Gavin, J. (2018). Revenge pornography: The influence of perpetrator-victim sex, observer sex and observer sexting experience on perceptions of seriousness and responsibility. *Journal of Criminal Psychology, 8*(2), 162–172. https://doi.org/10.1108/JCP-05-2017-0024

Starr, T. S., & Lavis, T. (2018). Perceptions of revenge pornography and victim blame. *International Journal of Cyber Criminology, 12*(2), 427–438. https://doi.org/10.5281/zenodo.3366179

Ricciardelli, R., & Adorjan, M. (2019). 'If a girl's photo gets sent around, that's a way bigger deal than if a guy's photo gets sent around': Gender, sexting, and the teenage years. *Journal of Gender Studies, 28*(5), 563–577. https://doi.org/10.1080/09589236.2018.1560245

Ringrose, J., Harvey, L., Gill, R., & Livingstone, S. (2013). Teen girls, sexual double standards and 'sexting': Gendered value in digital image exchange. *Feminist Theory, 14*(3), 305–323. https://doi.org/10.1177/1464700113499853

Trottier, D., Benbouriche, M., & Bonneville, V. (2021). A meta-analysis on the association between rape myth acceptance and sexual coercion perpetration. *The Journal of Sex Research, 58*(3), 375–382. https://doi.org/10.1080/00224499.2019.1704677

Van Ouytsel, J., Punyanunt-Carter, N. M., Walrave, M., & Ponnet, K. (2020a). Sexting within young adults' dating and romantic relationships. *Current Opinion in Psychology, 36*, 55–59. https://doi.org/10.1016/j.copsyc.2020.04.007

Van Ouytsel, J., Walrave, M., De Marez, L., Vanhaelewyn, B., & Ponnet, K. (2020b). Sexting, pressured sexting and image-based sexual abuse among a weighted-sample of heterosexual and LGB-youth. *Computers in Human Behavior, 117*. https://doi.org/10.1016/j.chb.2020.106630

Voelpel, S. C., Eckhoff, R. A., & Forster, J. (2008). David against Goliath? Group size and bystander effects in virtual knowledge sharing. *Human Relations, 61*(2), 271–295. https://doi.org/10.1177/0018726707087787

Zvi, L., & Shechory Bitton, M (2021). Perceptions of victim and offender culpability in non-consensual distribution of intimate images. *Psychology, Crime & Law, 27*(5), 427–442. https://doi.org/10.1080/1068316X.2020.1818236

CHAPTER 4

Time to Take Action: Barriers and Facilitators

Abstract While there is extensive research exploring factors that act to facilitate or hinder bystander intervention in sexual violence contexts, there is limited research on these factors in the context of image-based sexual abuse. In this chapter, we report on the survey and focus group data from the Image-Based Sexual Abuse and Bystander Intervention Study relating to actual and perceived experiences of witnessing and intervening in image-based sexual abuse contexts. This includes detailing findings around whether participants reported having witnessed image-based sexual abuse, and if so, whether they said or did anything (and details of what they said or did, where relevant). We also report on the factors that act to facilitate or hinder the perceived likelihood of bystander intervention in hypothetical scenarios, such as the nature of the relationship between parties, fear to personal safety, the role of other bystanders, and beliefs regarding the laws on image-based sexual abuse.

Keywords Image-based sexual abuse · Bystander · Intervention · Facilitators · Barriers · Law

Introduction

As discussed in Chapter 1, there is limited research on how often people witness and/or intervene in image-based sexual abuse incidents. Much of the research on witnessing image-based sexual abuse has been undertaken in Australia and the United Kingdom, with one Australian study finding that one in five participants witnessed image-based sexual abuse, and of these, four in ten did not take any action (Office of the eSafety Commissioner, 2017). Another study across Australia, New Zealand, and the United Kingdom found that of the participants who had witnessed image-based sexual abuse, only 46% had intervened in some way (Powell et al., 2020). Hypothetical studies examining bystander facilitators to intervention in image-based sexual abuse incidents have found that the perceived likelihood of intervention increases where participants feel a greater sense of responsibility, safety, and empathy (for the victim-survivor), as well as receiving benefits from intervention (Mainwaring et al., 2024). Another study from the United Kingdom described the types of actions participants may take, including supporting the victim-survivor, taking action against the perpetrator, and taking justice-related actions, such as collecting evidence of the abuse or encouraging the victim-survivor to report to the police (Mainwaring et al., 2023b). There remains a gap in knowledge of how often people witness image-based sexual abuse, how often they intervene, and what the barriers and facilitators are to intervention—in both real examples and hypothetical scenarios.

In this chapter, we report on actual and perceived experiences of bystander intervention in image-based sexual abuse contexts, as well as the barriers and facilitators that may impact intervention, drawing from both the survey and focus group data.

Witnessing Image-Based Sexual Abuse

In the survey, participants were asked whether they had witnessed, or become aware of, someone engaging in seven different forms of image-based sexual abuse: taking, sharing, uploading, threatening to share, downblousing, upskirting, and other (see Table 4.1). Overall, 64.1% of the sample had witnessed one or more forms of image-based sexual abuse, with the sharing of intimate images being the most frequent (46.1%) and 'other' (e.g. unsolicited 'dick pic' or 'twat shot') being the least frequent (13.9%).

Table 4.1 Experiences witnessing image-based sexual abuse, % (n)

	Overall (n = 245)	Gender		Sexuality	
		Female (n = 161)	Male (n = 73)	LGBQI+ (n = 62)	Hetero (n = 183)
Taking	20.0% (49)	21.1% (34)	17.8% (13)	16.1% (10)	21.3% (39)
Sharing	46.1% (113)	44.1% (71)	50.7% (37)	45.2% (28)	46.4% (85)
Uploading	28.6% (70)	29.2% (47)	28.8% (21)	33.9% (21)	26.8% (49)
Threatening	29.4% (72)	31.7% (51)	23.3% (17)	33.9% (21)	27.9% (51)
Downblousing	22.9% (56)	26.1% (42)	15.1% (11)	17.7% (11)	24.6% (45)
Upskirting	16.7% (41)	18.6% (30)	12.3% (9)	19.4% (12)	15.8% (29)
Other	13.9% (34)	14.3% (23)	12.3% (9)	19.4% (12)	12.0% (22)
Any	64.1% (157)	63.4% (102)	67.1% (49)	72.6% (45)	61.2% (112)

Note Gender comparisons utilise a slightly smaller sample (*n* = 234) because there were insufficient non-binary, transgender, or other gender identity participants (*n* = 11) for statistical analyses

The experiences of witnessing image-based sexual abuse were generally similar for female and male participants, as well as for LGBQI+ and heterosexual participants. However, female participants (26.1%) were more likely than male participants (15.1%) to have witnessed someone photographing or videoing another person's cleavage without that person's permission (i.e. downblousing), and LGBQI+ participants (72.6%) were more likely than heterosexual participants (61.2%) to have witnessed 'any' form of image-based sexual abuse.

Although our data did not permit an accurate estimation of frequency (because of the scale we used), we were able to generate averages for those participants who witnessed each of the seven different forms of image-based sexual abuse (see Table 4.2). Furthermore, five of the seven averages were between the second (2 times) and third (3 times) points on the scale, with the sharing of intimate images being the most frequently witnessed, between two and three times (2.44), and downblousing and upskirting being the least frequently witnessed, between one and two times (both 1.88).

The frequencies of witnessing image-based sexual abuse were generally similar for female and male participants, as well as for LGBQI+ and heterosexual participants. However, LBGQI+ participants (2.73) experienced witnessing downblousing more frequently than heterosexual participants (1.67).

Table 4.2 Frequency of witnessing image-based sexual abuse, M (SD)

	Overall	Gender		Sexuality	
		Female	Male	LGBQI+	Hetero
Taking	2.04 (1.38)	1.88 (1.25)	2.46 (1.71)	2.30 (1.49)	1.97 (1.37)
Sharing	2.44 (1.51)	2.38 (1.44)	2.59 (1.64)	2.64 (1.59)	2.38 (1.49)
Uploading	2.21 (1.59)	2.11 (1.48)	2.57 (1.83)	2.00 (1.45)	2.31 (1.65)
Threatening	2.03 (1.35)	2.06 (1.33)	2.18 (1.51)	1.86 (1.42)	2.10 (1.33)
Downblousing	1.88 (1.40)	1.83 (1.36)	1.91 (1.45)	2.73 (1.85)	1.67 (1.21)
Upskirting	1.88 (1.40)	1.87 (1.43)	1.67 (1.00)	2.33 (1.67)	1.69 (1.26)
Other	2.29 (1.64)	2.43 (1.75)	2.00 (1.50)	2.50 (1.78)	2.18 (1.59)

Note Measured via a 6-point scale ranging from 1 'no' to 6 '5+ times'. Consistent with Table 4.1, overall and sexuality comparisons utilise the full sample ($n = 245$), but gender comparisons utilise a slightly smaller sample ($n = 234$)

MOST RECENT WITNESS EXPERIENCE

Of the 157 survey participants who reported witnessing one or more of seven unwanted behaviours (each of which represented a different form of image-based sexual abuse), 149 provided further information about their most recent experience. Of these, 12.1% ($n = 18$) reported witnessing taking only and 54.4% ($n = 81$) reported witnessing sharing only. Additionally, 15.4% ($n = 23$) reported witnessing two forms of image-based sexual abuse (i.e. taking and sharing, taking and threatening, or sharing and threatening), and 6.0% ($n = 9$) reported witnessing all three forms of image-based sexual abuse (i.e. taking, sharing, and threatening).

When asked how strongly they experienced nine different feelings in response to witnessing the most recent image-based sexual abuse incident, participants felt 'somewhat' uncomfortable ($M = 4.07$) and 'somewhat' sorry for the victim-survivor ($M = 4.06$). They were also 'not at all' to 'not really' okay with it ($M = 1.69$) and found it 'not at all' to 'not really' funny ($M = 1.45$) (see Table 4.3).

Regarding gender comparisons, female participants were significantly more likely than male participants to report feeling uncomfortable ($M = 4.24$ vs. $M = 3.52$), annoyed ($M = 4.13$ vs. $M = 3.10$), and angry at the perpetrator ($M = 4.06$ vs. $M = 3.07$). Female participants were also more likely to feel sorry for the victim-survivor ($M = 4.14$ vs. $M = 3.83$) and bad about the situation ($M = 4.02$ vs. $M = 3.60$). In contrast, male participants were significantly more likely than female participants to be

Table 4.3 Feelings about most recent experience, M (SD)

	Overall	Gender		Sexuality	
		Female	Male	LGBQI+	Hetero
Uncomfortable	4.07 (1.18)	4.24 (1.05)	3.52 (1.38)	4.29 (1.11)	3.98 (1.21)
Sorry	4.06 (1.14)	4.14 (1.09)	3.83 (1.27)	3.95 (1.17)	4.10 (1.13)
Bad about it	3.92 (1.19)	4.02 (1.15)	3.60 (1.33)	3.93 (1.26)	3.92 (1.18)
Annoyed	3.85 (1.23)	4.13 (1.06)	3.10 (1.36)	3.83 (1.19)	3.85 (1.25)
Angry	3.80 (1.33)	4.06 (1.17)	3.07 (1.49)	3.93 (1.39)	3.75 (1.31)
Not bothered	2.08 (1.26)	2.01 (1.28)	2.36 (1.21)	2.02 (1.39)	2.10 (1.21)
Okay with it	1.69 (1.03)	1.46 (0.81)	2.33 (1.26)	1.79 (1.16)	1.65 (0.97)
Funny	1.45 (0.93)	1.37 (0.85)	1.71 (1.13)	1.45 (0.83)	1.45 (0.97)
Other	1.78 (1.36)	1.76 (1.35)	1.90 (1.48)	1.43 (1.13)	1.92 (1.43)

Note Measured via a 5-point scale ranging from '1 not at all' to '5 very much'. Consistent with Table 4.1, overall and sexuality comparisons utilise the full sample ($n = 245$), but gender comparisons utilise a slightly smaller sample ($n = 234$)

okay with it (M = 2.33 vs. M = 1.46) and find it funny (M = 1.71 vs. M = 1.37). Male participants were also more likely to report not being bothered by it (M = 2.36 vs. M = 2.01). These findings support research conducted across Australia, New Zealand, and the United Kingdom in which male victim-survivors of image-based sexual abuse were more likely to label their experience as 'funny', while female victim-survivors were more likely to feel fearful and to report negative emotions (Henry et al., 2020; Powell et al., 2022). Feelings about their most recent witness experience were generally similar for LGBQI+ and heterosexual participants. However, LGBQI+ participants (M = 4.29) were more likely than heterosexual participants (M = 3.98) to feel uncomfortable, and heterosexual participants (M = 1.92) were more likely than LGBQI+ participants (M = 1.43) to report having 'other' feelings (e.g. fear for the victim-survivor's safety and concern that other people may be victimised).

Finally, when asked whether they said or did anything in response to their most recent experience witnessing image-based sexual abuse, 45.6% ($n = 68$) of participants indicated that they did. Male participants (52.4%, $n = 22$) were more likely than female participants (42.0%, $n = 42$), and heterosexual participants (49.5%, $n = 53$) were more likely than LGBQI+ participants (35.7%, $n = 15$) to report saying or doing something in response to their most recent experience witnessing image-based sexual abuse. Although much of the literature on bystander intervention in sexual violence contexts has found that women are more likely to perceive that they would intervene when witnessing sexual violence compared to men, with this also being borne out in research on image-based sexual abuse (Krieger, 2020; Powell et al., 2020), research exploring actual intervention behaviour tends to find no differences according to gender (Mainwaring et al., 2023b). The findings above are therefore interesting in that male participants were more likely than female participants to report that they said or did something when witnessing image-based sexual abuse.

PERCEPTIONS OF WITNESSING IMAGE-BASED SEXUAL ABUSE

Survey participants were presented with one of eight versions of a scenario involving the non-consensual sharing of a sexual video, which differed according to the gender of the perpetrator, the gender of the victim-survivor, and the victim-survivor's initial consent to the sexual video. The purpose was to examine whether perpetrator gender, victim-survivor gender, and initial victim-survivor consent influence participants' behavioural intentions. Specifically, whether they would say or do anything, and what they would say and do (see Table 4.4 for two example scenarios).

Overall, participants were 'unsure' or would 'probably' say or do something ($M = 3.51$) if they became aware of what happened in the

Table 4.4   Example scenarios

Female perpetrator, male victim-survivor, self-recorded
Taylor has recently broken up with her boyfriend Sam, who is a good friend of yours. It was a nasty breakup with both sides posting rude comments about each other on Facebook and Instagram. When they were together, Sam sent Taylor a video of himself performing oral sex on her. Sometime after the breakup, Taylor sends the video to Sam's new girlfriend in order to embarrass him.

Male perpetrator, female victim-survivor, secretly recorded
Taylor has recently broken up with his girlfriend Sam, who is a good friend of yours. It was a nasty breakup with both sides posting rude comments about each other on Facebook and Instagram. When they were together, Taylor secretly recorded Sam performing oral sex on him. Sometime after the breakup, Taylor sends the video to Sam's new boyfriend in order to embarrass her.

---

scenario. Importantly, behavioural intentions were remarkably similar irrespective of perpetrator gender (woman M = 3.48 vs. M = 3.54 man), victim-survivor gender (woman M = 3.44 vs. M = 3.59 man), or initial victim-survivor consent (self-recorded M = 3.43 vs. M = 3.60 secretly recorded). Regarding what participants would say or do, 184 participants responded to the open-question and four themes were identified in the data. Most participants stated that they would confront the perpetrator (69.6%). Far fewer stated that they would report the behaviour (14.1%), support the victim-survivor (13.0%), or do something else (13.6%). A breakdown of gender differences in these actions is provided in Chapter 5.

When confronting the perpetrator, participants generally took one of three approaches. One approach was to admonish them, another was to ask them why they engaged in this behaviour, and the third was to inform them of the illegality of their behaviour. The following statements from participants provide some examples of these actions:

Tell her that what she did was unacceptable and she upset my friend. (P056 ADE M)

I would question Taylor [perpetrator] on why she did what she did. (P118 ADE F)

I'd tell him that he committed a criminal offence by sharing the material without permission. (P104 MEL F)

I would ask her why she felt the need to do something like that and remind her that she could potentially face criminal charges if she continues to share more images. (P102 CAN M)

When reporting the behaviour, participants referred to either reporting the behaviour themselves or encouraging the victim-survivor to report the behaviour:

Seriously consider reporting the matter to the police, and/or the university/workplace (if applicable). (P071 ADE M)

Tell Sam [victim-survivor] to contact the police about her spreading image. (P136 CAN F)

I would say to Sam [victim-survivor] go to the police. (P083 MEL F)

Give Sam [victim-survivor] support and discuss potential actions she could take. (P096 CAN NB)

Supporting the victim-survivor actions included participants informing the victim-survivor of what had happened, and providing emotional support:

A careful conversation about what you know has happened. (P061 CAN M)

Inform Taylor [victim-survivor] that the video has been shared. (P080 ADE F)

I would offer support and comfort to Sam [victim-survivor] and her new boyfriend. (P182 SYD F)

Provide any support I could for Sam [victim-survivor]. And ask Sam if there was anything I could do. (P221 ADE NB)

Finally, some participants stated that their action would be to do something else. Examples of this included not doing anything and distancing themselves from the perpetrator:

I wouldn't see it as my place to do so. (P073 SYD M)

If the video has already been sent then there is not much that can be done. (P186 SYD F)

I wouldn't associate with Taylor [perpetrator] after that. (P218 MEL Missing)

Stop the friendship [with the perpetrator]. (P243 MEL M)

The Role of Initial Victim-Survivor Consent

When survey participants were asked whether their view of the situation would change if the victim-survivor's initial consent to the sexual video had been different, participants felt 'unsure' (M = 2.99) (see Table 4.5). However, they were significantly more likely to believe their view would change when presented with the 'secretly recorded' scenario

Table 4.5 What if the victim-survivor's initial consent had been different, M (SD)

	Likelihood of viewing differently
Victim-survivor's initial consent	
Imagine sexual video self-recorded	3.89 (1.45)
Imagine sexual video secretly recorded	2.10 (1.23)
Overall	2.99 (1.61)

Note Measured via a 5-point scale ranging from '1 not at all' to '5 very much'

compared to the 'self-recorded' scenario. Specifically, participants believed their view would 'probably' change (M = 3.89) when presented with the 'secretly recorded' scenario and asked to imagine that the victim-survivor had recorded themselves performing a sexual act, but that their view would 'probably not' change (M = 2.10) when presented with the 'self-recorded' scenario and asked to imagine that the perpetrator had secretly recorded the victim-survivor performing a sexual act.

When participants believed their view would change if the victim-survivor's initial consent was different, they tended to focus on the cumulation of these actions as two crimes, as opposed to one. As these statements suggest:

> Not only did she share the video, the video was created without Sam's [victim-survivor's] consent too, which is an added level of betrayal. (P013 CAN F)

> It would be two consent violations instead of one, as well as a betrayal of trust both during and after the relationship. (P173 MEL NB)

> I would because recording secretly is an additional level of trust breached on top of sharing a video knowingly recorded in confidence. But both are still wrong. (P232 MEL M)

There were also some subtle and less subtle instances of victim-survivor blaming evident in participant responses when the video was self-recorded by the victim-survivor, and then later shared by the perpetrator, compared to when the video was secretly recorded by the perpetrator.

If Sam [victim-survivor] willingly participates in a video being made, then he should not be surprised if someone shares it because people can be cruel. But if the video was not agreed to by Sam, then in my view, he would not have to take any responsibility for it being shared. (P024 SYD F)

If that was the case [self-recorded], Sam [victim-survivor] would share more of the blame, however the main fault would still lie with Taylor [perpetrator]. (P092 MEL M)

If she had recorded the video of herself then she would have to take some responsibility, however Taylor [perpetrator] still shouldn't be allowed to share a video like that of someone without their permission. (P118 ADE F)

These findings are in keeping with the literature on victim-blaming and image-based sexual abuse, which finds that greater blame and responsibility is assigned to victim-survivors where images were self-taken (McKinlay & Lavis, 2020; Zvi & Shechory Bitton, 2021). In a survey conducted by Krieger (2020), victim-blaming attitudes were associated with lower intentions to help a victim-survivor in a hypothetical scenario. This also accords with the findings from our qualitative focus groups, as reported in Chapter 3.

However, when participants did not believe their view would change, they expressed the view that the harmful behaviour was the non-consensual sharing of the video, regardless of whether it had been self-recorded or secretly recorded. As these comments reflect:

I don't view any scenarios differently whether permission was received for filming or not. The images should not have been shared without Sam's [victim-survivor] permission. (P009 SYD F)

Who made the recording makes no difference. It's something private, and it shouldn't be shared. (P062 MEL M)

Even if both parties consented to filming the video, they did not consent to its distribution. (P197 ADE F)

These findings suggest that participants are aware of the harms associated with image-based sexual abuse behaviours; however, they also further reflect some of the discussion on victim-blaming and responsibility explored in Chapter 3, whereby the 'wrongness' of the perpetrator's behaviour in non-consensually sharing an image, or in this case, video, is perceived to be somewhat reduced when the victim-survivor is involved in the initial creation of the sexual imagery. We now move to considering the factors that influence bystander intervention drawing from the focus group data.

Factors Influencing Bystander Intervention

As outlined in Chapter 2, focus group participants were presented with hypothetical scenarios and asked a series of questions about the incidents (see Table 2.8 in Chapter 2 or Appendix Table A.1 for details of the scenarios). Participants identified several common barriers and facilitators to bystander intervention. Primarily, these related to the nature of the relationship between all parties (bystander, victim-survivor, perpetrator, and other people present); the perceived risk of intervening; the gender of the bystander, the victim-survivor, and the perpetrator; and the perceived likelihood of receiving support from other bystanders. In S1, perceptions of risk centred around the social implications of intervening, such as the reactions of both the perpetrator and the broader social group. These perceptions influenced participants' decisions regarding whether they would intervene at all, or within the group setting. In S2, there were several additional barriers that participants identified including ambiguity around what had occurred, the participants' views on the possible feelings of the victim-survivor, and any perceived power imbalances between the perpetrator and the bystander, such as age, physicality, and perpetrator state of mind.

Nature of Relationships as a Facilitator

Previous research on factors that influence bystander intervention in incidents of sexual violence has found that there is no clear association for the relationship between bystander and perpetrator with the likelihood of intervening (see Mainwaring et al., 2023a). Some studies have shown that bystanders are more likely to intervene or confront the perpetrator if it is someone they know, but that they may be less likely to provide support to the victim-survivor or engage with external resources, such as the police (Bennett et al., 2017; Katz & Nguyen, 2016; Palmer et al., 2018). In this study, the nature of the relationship between the bystander and the perpetrator was reported as both a facilitator and a barrier to intervention. In S1, focus group participants identified that the closeness of the relationship between themselves and the perpetrator could act as a potential facilitator to intervention. As one participant explained:

> If they were a close friend I'd definitely say, 'This is not appropriate'. (FG10 ADE F1)

One of the reasons identified for intervening if the perpetrator was a close friend was a perceived reduction in risk to personal safety or the likelihood of a negative outcome resulting from intervention. As the following participant explained, they would feel better able to intervene if the perpetrator was a close friend, as the level of friendship could act as a buffer against any negative consequences of saying or doing something:

> Is Kai [perpetrator], like, a close friend or is he just an acquaintance? Because that would change my reaction too. ... because, like, friends are friends. You can say whatever, and life is good. Like, there's that level of, trust or unconditional love, friendship. ... With an acquaintance, it's kind of like, you're kind of expendable. I don't need you in my friendship circle. You can just go. So, there's the difference between the two. (FG7 SYD F1)

When participants agreed that they would take action to intervene, the nature of the relationship between the bystander and the perpetrator was also discussed as impacting the type of action they would take. As one participant explained, 'it all comes down to what type of relationship you have with that person ... and that relationship dynamic'. (FG2 SYD F2)

In S1, the attitude of the perpetrator was identified as a key facilitator of intervention, particularly where they were making fun of the victim-survivor or overtly sexualising them:

> If she [the perpetrator] started pointing at certain parts of the photo and laughing at it or making comments about it ... I would say, 'I don't think you're supposed to show me that. I don't want to see it'. (FG4 ADE F1)

> The context of how he [the perpetrator] talks about it. If it was – yeah, it's kind of hard to explain, but if he was sort of bragging or making it clear

that, 'ha ha, I've got this', in a certain way, over perhaps just a discussion of the image, I'd say something. (FG8 ADE M1)

The type of intervention proposed by participants also differed according to the perpetrator's tone and attitude. As one participant observed:

> If she's sort of like, maybe distressed about it or kind of in shock, like, 'Someone sent me this, I don't want to deal with it', she's sort of already upset about everything, I'd be a lot more gentle with my words and saying, 'Hey, maybe don't show that. But I definitely understand that's not okay to be receiving things like that and that's not cool'. But if she's sort of like laughing about it, like, 'Ha! Look at this dick pic! What a joke!' It's easier for me to be like, 'Hey, hey. Calm down. That's not really cool. Just keep it to yourself'. It changes the way I [would] say it to her. (FG2 ADE F2)

Furthermore, empathy for the victim-survivor and the nature of the relationship between the bystander and the victim-survivor were key factors in facilitating intervention. As one participant expressed:

> I feel like if that was you yourself, you wouldn't want someone else sharing it, especially not to their friends, because then they've seen it, they've got a copy, they can spread it, and it's just like a never-ending cycle of who has the photo, and where it's going. So, kind of empathy with Arjun [victim-survivor], and his privacy. (FG3 ADE F2)

In S2, participants were asked whether their preparedness to intervene would change if Alex [victim-survivor] was their friend. Overwhelmingly, this question was responded to in the affirmative, with all participants indicating that it would increase their willingness to intervene, whether that involved telling Alex it occurred or confronting the perpetrator. This was largely because participants described feeling the need to defend their friend if they were being victimised. Further, participants felt that knowing the victim-survivor would remove any uncertainty or ambiguity over whether the victim-survivor would want them to intervene:

> I'd be more willing to, like, approach him [the perpetrator] if it was, like, my friend [the victim-survivor] that I was trying to defend and then if she didn't want me to, like, because then I could – because I would know her, I'd know how she would react. (FG2 SYD F1)

> If it was my friend [the victim-survivor], if it was someone I knew, 100%
> I would say something to Lou [perpetrator] because I have a personal
> connection. (FG8 ADE F4)

These findings support previous research around bystander intervention and sexual violence more broadly, which has found that a close relationship with the victim-survivor is linked to a greater willingness to intervene (see Mainwaring et al., 2023a for review). Research suggests that people may have greater empathy, sense of responsibility, and sense of loyalty or obligation towards their friends, which may lead to a greater willingness to intervene (Gable et al., 2021; Katz et al., 2015). Further, participants in the current study suggested that they would be better able to identify if their friend required assistance, which supports previous research that indicates friends may be better able to provide signals that they are in trouble and need assistance (Pugh et al., 2016).

Nature of Relationships as a Barrier

While there is some evidence that the relationship between the bystander and perpetrator can facilitate bystander intervention in sexual violence incidents, other studies have found that it may have the reverse effect by acting as a hindrance to intervention (Butler et al., 2017), or by impacting on how the bystander might intervene (Wamboldt et al., 2019). Some focus group participants in the current study similarly suggested that the 'nature of the friendship' (FG4 ADE M2) would be a potential barrier to intervening. For instance, participants described that they may not feel comfortable saying something and being the person 'telling off your friend' (FG6 ADE F1). As one participant reflected:

> Because you don't want possibly to be seen as the morality police, or the
> person who's saying, because it's effectively a form of sanction, you're sort
> of saying, I don't think this is appropriate. And whether you want to be
> seen as the person who pipes up and says, 'hi, me in the corner, I don't
> think that's appropriate'. (FG3 ADE F1)

For some participants, intervention would require overcoming the fear of conflict with the perpetrator:

It would be fear of creating some sort of conflict. ... It could destroy the relationship between me and the person. And ultimately, if I were to say something it would have to be overcoming that. (FG8 ADE F2)

This was of particular concern for participants who felt intervention might impact the friendship, for example, that it could 'jeopardise the trust between us' (FG 6 ADE F3), or because intervention could result in the person 'becoming annoyed and then they're going to be really mad at you' (FG7 ADE F2). Another focus group (FG5 ADE) identified not wanting to hurt or embarrass their friend as a barrier to intervention:

M1: I'm just thinking through the bloke-to-bloke dynamic again. He's my mate. He's just done something particularly stupid. A lot of my mates have done things which are particularly stupid. Do I embarrass them there and then? No.

M2: I don't think it gets you anywhere. ...

M3: You don't need to publicly shame him at that point, because I don't think it achieves anything.

Concerns about the breakdown of the relationship between the bystander and the perpetrator were further discussed in another focus group (FG7 SYD):

F3: Yeah, and also, you don't want to break that, like, relationship with Kai [perpetrator] and stuff because friendship, you've probably been like friends for years now. You don't want to sacrifice it.

F2: To go behind his back, yeah.

Reflecting the views expressed earlier that being a close friend of the perpetrator would act as a facilitator to intervention, some participants noted that if they were not a close friend of the perpetrator, this would act as a barrier to intervention:

If it was someone I wasn't as close to I'd probably be a bit not sure what the boundaries were within that relationship. (FG10 ADE F2)

Sometimes it just depends on how close a friend, like if I was friends with Sarah [perpetrator], is she my best friend, or just my friend? Sometimes it's really scary to speak up about how you feel if they're not that close. (FG3 ADE F2)

I think if I didn't know [the perpetrator] at all it would be a bit, maybe a bit weird for me to approach him out of the blue and be like, 'Hey what's the deal with this photo?'. (FG10 ADE M2)

Several participants felt that if there were people in the group who were closer friends with the perpetrator, then the responsibility for intervening would shift to them, in a sense, diffusing their responsibility (Darley & Latané, 1968):

If I wasn't as close of a friend within that broad group of friends or whatever, I feel like it would be another person who's closer to that person – it would be their responsibility to do that. (FG10 ADE M2)

This view was further discussed in one of the focus groups (FG10 ADE):

M3: It could be that maybe people who are closer to both of them would handle it and I wouldn't need to insert myself into the situation.

M4: Yeah, that's a good point, I think if there are other people around who were closer ... I might be inclined to think, well they are probably going to talk to her about it.

In relation to S2, participants primarily discussed the nature of the relationship between the victim-survivor and perpetrator as creating a barrier to intervention. Participants discussed that they might be less likely to intervene if they perceived that the victim-survivor and perpetrator knew each other, for example, if they appeared to be friends or partners:

If they were friends, it's sort of like, I'm going to ruin their friendship – even though he's already ruined it, because he took the photo. I think I'd find it a little harder to stand up to him, or even just pull her aside once she gets off the train, and be like, 'hey did you know he just did this?'. Or like, 'is this a thing, a friendship thing that you do?'. ... I think I'd just find it more difficult, because she might take his side, be like, he would never do that, he's my friend, what are you saying? (FG3 ADE F2)

If they appeared to be partners, if I could glean that from the way they were talking or interacting I'd be less likely to say something just because you don't know their dynamic. (FG7 MEL F1)

I reckon if I got the impression that they already knew each other, I'd kind of – I'd still think it's bad, but honestly, I'd probably just sort of think not my business and keep out of it. (FG8 ADE F1)

Where participants did reflect on the nature of their own relationship with the perpetrator, they mentioned feeling that if they knew the perpetrator, it might be uncomfortable to confront them in that public space:

If you knew Lou [perpetrator], I mean that could be a super awkward situation, if you actually know this person, and now I know they're a creeper, but is this the appropriate place for me to say anything about it? (FG3 ADE F1)

In S1, in addition to the nature of the relationship with the perpetrator being a barrier, some participants noted that the nature of their relationship with the broader social group or the group dynamics was a potential barrier to intervention, reflecting Darley and Latané's (1968) bystander effect theory—step three, social influence (see Chapter 1 for an outline of this theory). As one participant observed:

I think it depends on the way that it's brought up. Sometimes you might feel social pressure not to say something especially if there's an environment of – as horrible as this sounds – like what they're saying, 'Oh my God check out what I got', sort of thing. (FG7 ADE F2)

Participants felt that it would be difficult to intervene if the group was largely supportive of the perpetrator showing the image. In these instances, participants described that they might choose not to say something, or that they may say something to the perpetrator later in private. As discussed in one focus group (FG4 ADE):

F1: I think if we were around a bunch of people and Sarah [perpetrator] showed the photo and everyone else is like, 'That's so funny' or I don't know, I think that would make it harder for me to speak.

F3: Yeah, if there were a bunch of people supporting Sarah, I think it would make it harder for me to say no.

F1: Yeah, if everyone was supporting her it would make it harder for me to say, 'No that's not good'.

These findings may be indicative of pluralistic ignorance, whereby there are discrepancies between perceived and actual norms around bystander intervention. Research suggests that people may perceive that their peers would be less likely to support bystander intervention than those peers are in reality (Fabiano et al., 2003; Kroshus, 2018). Thus, in the current study, participants may perceive the group to be supportive of showing the image, even if the group may not actually be supportive. The research shows that perceptions of the attitudes of others can influence behaviours more than one's own attitudes (Brown & Messman-Moore, 2010; Kroshus, 2018). This is an area that has not been studied in relation to bystander intervention in the context of image-based sexual abuse and which may warrant further attention.

Perceptions of Safety and Risk as a Barrier

In line with much research on bystander intervention (Fischer et al., 2011; Hamby et al., 2016; Lodge & Frydenberg, 2005), focus group participants recognised the potential cost of 'putting yourself in a position of risk' (FG1 ADE M1) as a key barrier to saying or doing something in both scenarios. However, the perceived risks varied between S1 and S2, with participants in S1 primarily identifying the social risks of intervening, and participants in S2 primarily focusing on the potential risks to personal or physical safety posed by intervening.

In S1, participants were very conscious of how intervention might be perceived by their friendship group, and any negative perceptions or consequences were acknowledged as a key barrier to saying or doing anything. This reflects Burn's (2009) research, discussed in Chap. 1, on how a fear of negative evaluation or 'evaluation apprehension' can act as a barrier to intervention, including concerns that others will view intervention as unnecessary or inappropriate. Participants described being 'the one that deviates from the herd … the black sheep' (FG2 CAN F2) by intervening in a group setting as a key barrier to intervention. The social risks for participants included potentially negative reactions from both the perpetrator and the broader social group, which, as mentioned in the previous section, may be reflective of pluralistic ignorance:

> So, if it's in a group situation sort of, you want to – if the rest of the group all sides with him, then you feel sort of bad if you're the only one commenting. They'll all judge you a bit for that. (FG8 ADE F1)

> If we're really honest, my opinion is that you would be, I think, a little bit nervous about calling it out straight away because you don't want to be seen as the negative person or the – whatever the word is – the negative person … the 'killjoy', yeah. … So, there's a fear of standing up. (FG5 ADE F5)

Physical safety did not seem to be a dominant concern in relation to S1, as participants noted there would be a greater level of comfort from being in a group situation surrounded by friends. However, as the following comments reflect, some participants raised the issue of safety in relation to being surrounded by a group of the perpetrator's friends, rather than their own friends:

> … if I felt threatened or couldn't guarantee my safety for confronting Kai [perpetrator] or even Kai's friends, if it was in a situation that I didn't feel [safe] – then that would be a big barrier. (FG7 MEL F3)

Personal and physical safety was repeatedly identified in the discussions of S2. Many participants described needing to assess their own safety before intervening. In many cases, an assessment of the situation as potentially affecting their personal safety outweighed participants' desires to intervene or help the victim-survivor. As several participants reflected:

> Even though you want to help her, you also don't want to put yourself at more risk. (FG2 ADE F3)

> What I'm thinking in my head is that particularly if you confront Lou [perpetrator], and the situation gets heated, you could be putting yourself in a position of risk. (FG1 ADE M2)

> I'm not going to put myself at risk. (FG7 ADE F1)

Participants were concerned that intervening in the situation could result in the perpetrator becoming physically violent. Previous studies have consistently shown that fear of getting hurt or injured is a barrier to intervention in sexual violence contexts (Hoxmeier et al., 2019; Lamb & Attwell, 2019). In the current study, these feelings were strongly influenced by participants' perceptions of the perpetrator. For example, if the participants imagined the perpetrator to be physically intimidating, this influenced their preparedness to intervene:

> I would say safety. I don't know if they're going to attack me. ... I don't know if they're going to bash me. ... You just don't know, so I'd be a bit worried about that. (FG1 MEL F1)

> I'd be thinking if I say something to Lou [perpetrator], is she going to freak her nut at me in order to turn the attention away from what she's done. (FG10 ADE F2)

Perceptions of intimidation were largely linked to Lou's [perpetrator] physical appearance:

> If Lou looks like he can fight, then I don't think I would be able to take him on. (FG4 ADE F1)

> If Lou was six foot four and built like an ox, that would definitely be a barrier. (FG10 MEL M2)

> I was just going to say, let's say he's some massive body-builder dude who could like, crush a car. (FG2 ADE M2)

The perpetrator's age also factored into participants' preparedness to intervene. Participants made comments such as Lou's [perpetrator] age 'would make me almost nervous, someone older than you' (FG10 ADE F4) and 'the fact that he's 30, and I'm 19, that's pretty scary' (FG 3 ADE F2). Others explained:

> If Lou's a 30-year-old man it might be more difficult to confront Lou. (FG10 ADE M2)

> Even if he was a thinner guy, I would probably not stand up against an older man. (FG5 ADE F2)

Others pointed to age as an indicator of authority and a clear power imbalance that would be difficult to overcome in order to intervene:

> The fact that Lou is so much older than me – like, I really quite struggle with standing up to authority, and people being my senior is a big thing for me: oh, they're older, they're the boss of you. I don't think I could have the strength to go up to a 30-year-old woman and say, 'Hey, what you're doing is wrong', as a 20-year-old girl. If it was a 12-year-old boy, I would be like, get out of here, because you're his senior. (FG6 ADE F4)

> It's scary and also just like, if I say anything, she's just going to be like, 'Who do you think you are? You are this young girl; you cannot tell me at all what to do'. (FG6 ADE F3)

> When you are a young woman, it can be that you're just not taken seriously, you're just this tiny little voice. (FG3 ADE F2)

The threat to safety as a barrier was commonly discussed in contexts in which there was a sense that the bystander may not have the support of other people. Where there was a perception that others would support the bystander, as discussed in the next section, this became a key facilitator to intervention in both scenarios.

Support of Other Bystanders as a Facilitator

In a recent systematic review of bystander intervention in sexual violence contexts, researchers found that the presence of other bystanders is one of the most researched aspects of bystander intervention (Mainwaring et al., 2023b). However, the review found that whether this acted to facilitate or hinder bystander intervention remains unclear, with some studies finding that the presence of other bystanders facilitates intervention, while others finding it to be a barrier to intervention (Mainwaring et al., 2023b). In the context of image-based sexual abuse, the role of bystanders in acting to facilitate or hinder intervention similarly remains unclear (Mainwaring, 2023). In our focus groups, participants generally believed that having support or potential backup from other bystanders, whether other passengers or a friend on the train, or being among a friendship group, was a key facilitator for them intervening:

> If it's a pretty busy train and there's other people noticing as well, so it's not just me, that would give me more incentive to actually do something. (FG10 ADE M1)

> If it was on a public train as well and others heard the conversation, I would hope that people with good morals would interject as well. (FG3 MEL F1)

Some participants acknowledged that they would intervene only if they knew other people on the train. For example, one participant claimed:

> If I had a friend with me, I feel like I'd be more inclined to say something because I'm, like, I've got backup, it's okay. But if I was by myself, I tend to mind my own business a bit more. So as much as I want to do something, I feel like I wouldn't have the courage to do it. (FG10 SYD F1)

In discussing S2, another participant said that having other people present on the train would give them 'the perspective that it might be safer … to say something to Lou [the perpetrator]' (FG1 SYD F3). However, some participants described how having other people present would act as a deterrent for the perpetrator in continuing their behaviour or escalating the situation. As the following participant explained:

> I would say to someone else, if I was alone, another passenger, I'd be, like, 'Hey, this guy's being real creepy. Can you help me to intervene?' Because then it's kind of like the psychological thing for him, where there's more than one person confronting him, so then he feels uncomfortable and stops. (FG2 ADE M2)

Some participants suggested that having other people present would also be useful as they may be compelled or feel pressure to intervene if another bystander took the first action:

> How many people are on the train? If it's a very quiet train there's more risk that that person could snap or do something bad. But if it's packed, I think there would be pressure from other people who would help to stand up against them. (FG8 SYD F2)

Beliefs Regarding Image-Based Sexual Abuse Laws

One of the further factors we sought to explore was whether beliefs regarding image-based sexual abuse laws would influence participants' likelihood to intervene. To our knowledge, no other study has examined this variable as a barrier or facilitator to bystander intervention. We first gauged participant beliefs in the survey, where they were asked to indicate whether they believe image-based sexual abuse (1) *is currently a crime* in their state and (2) *should be a crime* in their state. Both sets of questions considered the following image-based sexual abuse behaviours: take, share, upload and threaten to share. The pattern of responses was the same across both questions, with participants most likely to believe it is a crime, and should be a crime, to upload an intimate image online, and least likely to believe it is a crime, and should be a crime, to threaten to share an intimate image (see Tables 4.6 and 4.7).

More than half of participants believed *it is a crime* to upload (66.1%), take (57.6%), and/or share (51.4%) an intimate image of someone without their permission. However, only 38.8% of participants believed *it is a crime* to threaten to share an intimate image of someone. Regarding beliefs of whether image-based sexual abuse *should be a crime*, the average level of agreement was high across all forms of image-based sexual abuse. All averages were between the fourth and fifth points of the scale, suggesting that participants believed it should 'probably' or 'definitely' be a crime to upload (4.82), take (4.64) share (4.60), and/or threaten to share (4.51) an intimate image of someone without their permission.

Table 4.6   Beliefs regarding whether image-based sexual abuse is a crime, % (n)

	Overall (n = 245)	Gender		Sexuality	
		Female (n = 161)	Male (n = 73)	LGBQI+ (n = 62)	Hetero (n = 183)
Take	57.6% (141)	56.5% (91)	58.9% (43)	67.7% (42)	54.1% (99)
Share	51.4% (126)	55.3% (89)	46.6% (34)	43.5% (27)	54.1% (99)
Upload	66.1% (162)	67.1% (108)	64.4% (47)	66.1% (41)	66.1% (121)
Threaten to share	38.8% (95)	39.1% (63)	41.1% (30)	37.1% (23)	39.3% (72)

Note Gender comparisons utilise a slightly smaller sample ($n = 234$) because there were insufficient non-binary, transgender, or other gender identity participants ($n = 11$) for statistical analyses

Table 4.7 Beliefs regarding whether image-based sexual abuse should be a crime, M (SD)

		Gender		Sexuality	
	Overall	Female	Male	LGBQI+	Hetero
Take	4.64 (0.72)	4.73 (0.64)	4.45 (0.83)	4.66 (0.73)	4.58 (0.69)
Share	4.60 (0.76)	4.71 (0.68)	4.36 (0.87)	4.65 (0.72)	4.47 (0.86)
Upload	4.82 (0.58)	4.87 (0.55)	4.70 (0.62)	4.83 (0.57)	4.79 (0.60)
Threaten to share	4.51 (0.81)	4.57 (0.81)	4.41 (0.85)	4.49 (0.84)	4.56 (0.72)

Note Measured via a 5-point scale ranging from 1 'definitely not' to 7 'definitely'. Consistent with Table 4.6, overall and sexuality comparisons utilise the full sample ($n = 245$), but gender comparisons utilise a slightly smaller sample ($n = 234$)

Regarding gender comparisons, beliefs of whether image-based sexual abuse *is a crime* did not differ for female and male participants. However, there were small but consistent gender differences regarding beliefs of whether image-based sexual abuse *should be a crime*. Female participants reported significantly higher levels of agreement than male participants that it should be a crime to take (M = 4.73 vs. M = 4.45), share (M = 4.71 vs. M = 4.36), and upload (M = 4.87 vs. M = 4.70) an intimate image of someone without their permission (there was no significant gender difference for threatening to share an intimate image). Regarding sexuality comparisons, beliefs of whether image-based sexual abuse *is a crime* were generally similar for LGBQI+ and heterosexual participants. However, LGBQI+ participants (67.7%) were more likely than heterosexual participants (54.1%) to believe it is currently a crime to take intimate images of someone without their permission. Beliefs of whether image-based sexual abuse *should be a crime* did not differ between LGBQI+ and heterosexual participants.

Unsurprisingly, the focus group discussions mirrored these survey findings, revealing some confusion over whether the behaviours described in S1 did or should constitute a crime. The main point of contention for participants was the perceived difference in harm between showing the image to a group of friends in person, and distributing the image to a group of friends—whether by a social media or messaging app or uploading the image online—given the potential for that image to then be further shared beyond the friendship group. As some participants described:

I don't think it's a crime, because to me the thing that distinguishes it is that she hasn't published anything or distributed anything. I think that's a pretty clear divide between where you need a criminal response. (FG1 ADE M2)

I think it's in a private forum, she's not profiting from it. I don't see it as really, like she hasn't even asked for the picture. I don't really see it as being a crime. (FG1 ADE F1)

Because it's a closed group, the friends are close and it's a closed group. If she uploaded it online, it would have a different aspect of that where it would be shared among millions, so it would be something [worse]. It would have the face of a crime. (FG3 MEL F2)

The perceived differences in harm to the victim-survivor influenced why participants saw distributing the image to be 'worse' than showing the image. One focus group (FG4 MEL) reflected on this below, highlighting that distributing the image meant that there was more constancy to the harm experienced (see also McGlynn et al., 2021):

F2: If she shares it [online], it will be there forever. And, he will know, and she will know, and other people will know, and you can't really take it down.

F1: Yeah, I think something with that digital footprint – it can never get taken down. Whereas, like, me being like this [holds up phone] – like, yes, it's on my phone. But it's, like, a quick thing –

F2: It's in my memory, but it's just my memory.

F1: Sarah [the perpetrator] is the only one that has possession of that photo.

F3: You can't really do much damage to the person's image. Whereas, when it's online, people can store photos and use it against people in the future as well.

For some participants, the key issue was evidence, and the difficulty of proving that the image was shown, versus distributing and publishing the image through a Messenger app or online context where there might be 'more' evidence:

Showing is hard to, it's more hearsay, it's like, he did this, and then she did that, and then I saw it from there, and it's like, well, where's all the evidence? So, it would be really hard to prove. (FG3 ADE F2)

Even if it was a crime, like the evidence that would be needed to charge someone for that would be really difficult to obtain. (FG1 ADE F1)

After participants reflected on whether the act currently constituted an offence, they were then asked whether they thought it should be an offence. The presence or lack of consent was a key factor determining whether participants felt the behaviours should be a crime:

I think it should be a crime if there's no consent. Why people would question it should be a crime is because sharing of photos is so normalised. And for me, it's like, you can't take someone to someone's bedroom door and let them spy on your girlfriend, in the same way you can't show them things that she would consider private. So, the lack of consent for me is what sort of pushes it into a criminal area. (FG8 SYD F2)

I think it needs to all be a crime and I think it needs to be blanket because otherwise where does it stop? Like, even if socially it's kind of okay for him, might be okay for him to show a group of his friends in person, like where does it stop? So, if it's okay to show his friend, is it okay to show her mum, is it okay to show her boss? Like, where do you draw the line. So, I think you just have to make it blanket and say it's not okay to share it without consent. (FG7 SYD F4)

A similar view was presented by two participants in another focus group (FG1 SYD), who stated:

F2: I think it should be [a crime], especially if Maryam's [victim-survivor] sent something and it was supposed to be just between those two, and it shows something that's quite explicit, there's other ramifications for her as well. So, if he's breached that trust, it should be something that is illegal.

F1: Yeah, I agree. I think it should be illegal, if he didn't have consent to show [it].

While some participants felt that it should be a crime, the blurred distinction between showing and distributing the image was again a key factor shaping participants' views, with some describing distributing and showing people in person as 'two different things' (FG10 MEL M1), and distributing as 'the next step up' (FG1 MEL F1) from showing it to the group:

> Yeah, I don't think it should be illegal, because also at the same time, you have the issue of other people sending them I suppose, and I think it shouldn't – I think if someone publicises the image, if they put it online, that's a completely different story. But if they show you. If they keep it on their phone, I think it's very different showing them. But I don't agree with it. I mean, I don't think it's morally right. (FG4 CAN F2)

> Showing it is not as detrimental because those people, that group, can't then go on to disseminate it. (FG8 ADE M2)

Other participants focused on the intent of the person showing the image as a factor that would make it more (or less) likely to be a crime. As one participant claimed, 'I think if your girlfriend sends you a nude and you break up and you send it to everyone, that's definitely a crime, because that's wrong'. (FG6 ADE F3)

Some participants felt that criminalising the act would send a message to the community that such behaviour is not tolerated, but that, ultimately, it should be on the lower spectrum of offending behaviour:

> It should be one of those things that can be, could be a crime kind of thing. I mean it's like, technically, yes, but in many, many cases it should be treated as a bit trivial. (FG4 ADE M1)

Others focused on the harm caused to the victim-survivor as the key factor influencing whether it is, or should be, considered a crime:

> I certainly don't think it should be something that is criminalised, until it reaches a higher threshold of causing someone distress. (FG2 CAN M1)

While some participants recognised the harm of the act and questioned the 'morality' of showing the image, they felt that it should not be against the law. These participants described criminalising the act as 'kind of dramatic' (FG4 ADE F1) and 'a bit extreme' (FG4 SYD F1). When reflecting on the reasons, participants pointed to the act being 'morally wrong, but maybe not criminally wrong, ... just ethically wrong' (FG1 CAN F1). Linked to the victim-blaming discussion in Chapter 3, another participant claimed that the victim-survivor loses ownership of the image once it is sent, and therefore, it should not be an offence to show it to others with or without the person's consent:

> It shouldn't be breaking the law, because if someone gives me an apple, it's then my apple. And what I do with that apple is my decision. But the fact that in a digital world, someone gives you a picture, if they've given it to you like a gift, you can do what you want with it. (FG4 CAN M1)

In addition to attributing blame to the victim-survivor, in that they lose ownership of the image once it is sent, participants reflected on whether sending the image in the first place should itself be an offence. In this regard, they drew on discussions of the unsolicited image being a form of sexual harassment, but that there would need to be some distress element for the person receiving it, for it to constitute an offence:

> If it was part of something more broad, like either psychological abuse or sexual abuse ... There has to be that kind of negative affect on [the person receiving the image] otherwise it wouldn't – it wouldn't get reported and then it wouldn't work as a crime. (FG9 SYD F1)

> It is like sexual harassment ... because you don't want to open your phone and just see that unless you've asked for it. Because usually if you're doing that there should be consent between two people that you're okay with this. ... I don't want to get pictures. If it was me I wouldn't – and I haven't asked – I wouldn't be wanting to get pictures of males. So, there is a distressed element there but yeah, I think it should be a crime. (FG9 SYD F2)

Participants again reflected on the murky nature of consent and perception of the victim-survivor having some degree of responsibility in S1, compared with S2, which led to a broader consensus around the behaviour being a criminal act in S2. As this participant observed:

> Compare it to the first scenario, this is strictly wrong. There's no black or white. There's no shades of grey. This is clearly wrong. Your first context was a completely – he voluntarily took a photo of himself, and this is not the same thing. This is chalk and cheese. It's wrong on so many levels. (FG5 MEL M2)

It was evident that participants' perspectives and beliefs about whether the behaviour constituted an offence was a factor influencing their behaviour. This was particularly so in S1, where almost no participants suggested involving the police or another authority, and most felt that if they did intervene, it would be sufficient to simply talk to the perpetrator, tell the victim-survivor, or stop hanging around with the perpetrator. In S2, however, almost all participants agreed that the act of upskirting was an offence and should be treated as such. Nevertheless, the fact that participants believed the behaviour was illegal was not found to impact on their likelihood to intervene, or what action they would take. Instead, participants focused on the potential harm to the victim-survivor.

While very few participants suggested police intervention would be appropriate in S1, there was a view expressed that the police may not take the matter seriously:

A lot of people don't trust the way that the police and the courts handle this stuff. I'd trust reporting it to a women's WIRE [support, referrals and information for women] organisation or something, but not VicPol [Victoria Police]. VicPol's known to muck this stuff up and make women feel more traumatised. The whole thing of criminalising it is a huge broader issue, because that makes things worse normally for the victim. (FG5 MEL M2)

In discussing S2, many participants also stated that they would not report the behaviour to the police or encourage the victim-survivor to report to the police as a bystander intervention action. This decision was largely because of concerns raised about the effectiveness of the police in responding to this type of crime, again reflective of research in this field (Bond & Tyrell, 2021; Flynn, 2023; Flynn & Henry, 2021; Flynn et al., 2023b; Henry et al., 2018). In one focus group (FG1 ADE), for example, the following comments were made:

M1: I'm a bit sceptical that the police would do anything, myself. ... I'm a bit sceptical, and I guess that reflects me. I would say [to the victim-survivor], you may well report it, but I suspect it wouldn't go anywhere.

M2: And that weighs into what I said about not wanting to take agency away from Alex [victim-survivor]. Like, I especially don't want to subject them to something which is going to be really ineffective. The police say that they take this seriously, and you do hear about people getting arrested for this, but yeah.

F1: I don't think I've ever heard of someone getting arrested for taking a photo up someone's skirt. I feel like Crimestoppers might be more effective. I feel like the police wouldn't respond effectively if you dialled 000, because it's not a life-threatening thing.

Others similarly felt that the police would not take the crime seriously:

I can imagine some police might just go, 'Oh really? We've got way more important crimes to solve and deal with than that'. The perception of this type of incident may not be as serious as it should be. … It's hard enough to report a rape, let alone someone taking a photo up your skirt, so why would you bother? (FG10 ADE F2)

I'd be fairly cynical about what the police's response would be. … Would I encourage her to [report], I don't really think so. (FG4 ADE M1)

The police wouldn't take action against her [the perpetrator]. They'd just be like, 'Thanks', and not do anything about it. (FG9 SYD F1)

We explore the history of police discrimination and harassment of non-binary and transgender people as another barrier to seeking police support as an intervention mechanism in Chapter 5.

Some participants felt that the police would take the matter seriously, and that if the victim-survivor did not report it, there may be a risk of other people experiencing similar offending from the perpetrator in the future. This was a factor influencing their likelihood to report to police as a bystander action. As one participant explained, 'This could've been reported five times before on the train and they've never caught the person, and this report helps them get him' (FG1 CAN M1). Participants in another focus group (FG1 SYD) stated:

F1: I'd recommend she report it, for the benefit of other people I guess.

M1: Make a stand because it's wrong on every level.

F2: It starts off with that sort of thing, and then next thing you know they're creeping into somebody's house.

F1: It's her choice to report it, but I'd encourage her to do it. (FG1 SYD)

While recognising the importance of reporting such an offence, it was acknowledged by many participants that the difficulties of the court process may be a reason why Alex [victim-survivor] would not want to report to the police, and why they may not recommend reporting to the police:

> It would be probably very tough on Alex. She'd have to give evidence in court, and she might not be prepared to do that. And so, it's really up to her to decide what to do about it. (FG2 CAN F1)

> Some people would for various reasons not want to make a complaint and not want to go down that, because it's really not much fun being a victim in a criminal matter, having to go to court and everything else. (FG1 ADE M2)

Several participants expressed that they would want to inform police of the situation without involving Alex [victim-survivor]. Some of these participants felt that by not involving Alex, they could protect her from potential emotional distress from getting involved in the criminal justice system:

> I think in that situation I'd confront Lou [perpetrator] immediately and probably not involve Alex. Like, if I could confront Lou and get her to delete the photo, I'd probably never tell Alex it happened. Whereas if Lou didn't react and wouldn't delete the photo, yeah, I'm not sure if I'd tell Alex or not, but I'd probably go to the authorities after that. (FG8 ADE F1)

Others similarly indicated that they would involve the police as their bystander action regardless of Alex's [victim-survivor] views. However, their focus was on taking punitive measures against the perpetrator:

> You have to do something. Of course, if I saw something like this I would report if I saw some policeman near or someone near, of course. Doesn't matter what Alex thinks about it. It's about that other guy. (FG2 MEL F2)

These discussions further highlight the importance of having alternate avenues of support and justice available for victim-survivors of image-based sexual abuse which are not reliant on criminal law and the criminal justice system. While the law can play an important role in sending a clear message to the community that image-based sexual abuse is wrong, and it provides a mechanism for holding perpetrators accountable, deterring future offending and enabling victim-survivors to seek justice, legal responses alone will not be as effective as combining them with different non-legal options and education and prevention messaging (Flynn & Henry, 2021; Henry et al., 2019). Further, as the findings in this chapter show, belief or knowledge of laws around image-based sexual abuse is not sufficient alone to facilitate bystander intervention. It is therefore important to explore other factors that may facilitate positive bystander intervention in image-based sexual abuse contexts.

Conclusion

This chapter has presented findings relating to actual and perceived experiences of bystander intervention in image-based sexual abuse contexts. This included detailing findings around whether participants reported having witnessed image-based sexual abuse, and if so, whether they said or did anything (and details of what they said or did). We also considered some of the motivations behind taking action or not taking action reported in the survey for both actual and hypothetical incidents of witnessing image-based sexual abuse, and the various factors that influenced bystander intervention. The findings highlight the importance of the nature of the relationship between the parties and the role of other bystanders as both facilitators and barriers to intervention. The findings also demonstrate that fear to personal safety was a barrier, and that beliefs or knowledge regarding the laws on image-based sexual abuse play a much smaller role in influencing whether someone would intervene. In the next chapter, we explore the role that gender plays in bystander intervention, including shaping attitudes towards the victim-survivor and perpetrator. We also explore how different gendered assumptions and expectations influence decision-making in bystander contexts.

REFERENCES

Bennett, S., Banyard, V. L., & Edwards, K. M. (2017). The impact of the bystander's relationship with the victim and the perpetrator on intent to help in situations involving sexual violence. *Journal of Interpersonal Violence, 32*(5), 682–702. https://doi.org/10.1177/0886260515586373

Bond, E., & Tyrell, E. (2021). Understanding revenge pornography: A national survey of police officers and staff in England and Wales. *Journal of Interpersonal Violence, 36*(5–6), 2166–2181. https://doi.org/10.1177/086626051 8760011

Brown, A. L., & Messman-Moore, T. L. (2010). Personal and perceived peer attitudes supporting sexual aggression as predictors of male college students' willingness to intervene against sexual aggression. *Journal of Interpersonal Violence, 25*(3), 503–517. https://doi.org/10.1177/0886260509334400

Burn, S. M. (2009). A situational model of sexual assault prevention through bystander intervention. *Sex Roles: A Journal of Research, 60*(11–12), 779–792. https://doi.org/10.1007/s11199-008-9581-5

Butler, L., Ningard, H., Pugh, B., & Vander, V. T. (2017). Creepers, druggers, and predator ambiguity: The interactional construction of campus victimization and the university sex predator. *American Journal of Criminal Justice, 42*(4), 790–806. https://doi.org/10.1007/s12103-016-9383-1

Darley, J. M., & Latané, B. (1968). Bystander intervention in emergencies: Diffusion of responsibility. *Journal of Personality and Social Psychology, 8*(4, Pt. 1), 377–383. https://doi.org/10.1037/h0025589

Fabiano, P. M., Perkins, H. W., Berkowitz, A., Linkenbach, J., & Stark, C. (2003). Engaging men as social justice allies in ending violence against women: Evidence for a social norms approach. *Journal of American College Health, 52*(3), 105–112. https://doi.org/10.1080/0744848030959573

Fischer, P., Krueger, J., Greitemeyer, T., Vogrincic, C., Kastenmüller, A., Frey, D., Heene, M., Wicher, M., & Kainbacher, M. (2011). The bystander-effect: A meta-analytic review on bystander intervention in dangerous and non-dangerous emergencies. *Psychological Bulletin, 137*(4), 517–537. https://doi.org/10.1037/a0023304

Flynn, A. (2023). Image-based sexual abuse. In H. Pontell (Ed.), *Oxford research encyclopedia of criminology and criminal justice* (2nd ed.). Oxford University Press. https://doi.org/10.1093/acrefore/9780190264079.013.534

Flynn, A., & Henry, N. (2021). Image-based sexual abuse: An Australian reflection. *Women and Criminal Justice, 31*(4), 313–326. https://doi.org/10.1080/08974454.2019.1646190

Flynn, A., Cama, E., Powell, A., & Scott, A. J. (2023a). Victim-blaming and image-based sexual abuse. *Journal of Criminology, 56*(1), 7–15. https://doi.org/10.1177/26338076221135327

Flynn, A., Powell, A., & Hindes, S. (2023b). Policing technology-facilitated abuse. *Policing & Society, 33*(5), 572–592. https://doi.org/10.1080/104 39463.2022.2159400

Gable, S. C., Lamb, S., Brodt, M., & Atwell, L. (2021). Intervening in a "sketchy situation": Exploring the moral motivations of college bystanders of sexual assault. *Journal of Interpersonal Violence, 36*(1–2), NP311–NP334. https://doi.org/10.1177/0886260517730027

Hamby, S. L., Weber, M. C., Grych, J. H., & Banyard, V. (2016). What difference do bystanders make? The association of bystander involvement with victim outcomes in a community sample. *Psychology of Violence, 6*(1), 91–102. https://doi.org/10.1037/a0039073

Henry, N., Flynn, A., & Powell, A. (2018). Policing image-based sexual abuse: Stakeholder perspectives. *Police Practice and Research: An International Journal, 19*(6), 565–581. https://doi.org/10.1080/15614263.2018. 1507892

Henry, N., Flynn, A., & Powell, A. (2019). *Responding to revenge pornography: The scope, nature and impact of Australian criminal laws—A report to the Criminology Research Council.* Australian Institute of Criminology. Retrieved October 21, 2024, from https://www.aic.gov.au/sites/default/files/2020-05/CRG_08_15-16-FinalReport.pdf

Henry, N., McGlynn, C., Flynn, A., Johnson, K., Powell, A., & Scott, A. J. (2020). *Image-based sexual abuse: A study on the causes and consequences of non-consensual nude or sexual imagery.* Routledge.

Hoxmeier, J. C., O'Connor, J., & McMahon, S. (2019). 'She wasn't resisting': Students' barriers to prosocial intervention as bystanders to sexual assault risk situations. *Violence against Women, 25*(4), 485–505. https://doi.org/10. 1177/1077801218790697

Katz, J., & Nguyen, L. J. (2016). Bystander responses to risk for rape perpetrated by a friend, acquaintance, or stranger. *Journal of Aggression, Maltreatment & Trauma, 25*(6), 652–667. https://doi.org/10.1080/10926771.2016.118 5755

Katz, J., Pazienza, R., Olin, R., & Rich, H. (2015). That's what friends are for: Bystander responses to friends or strangers at risk for party rape victimization. *Journal of Interpersonal Violence, 30*(16), 2775–2792. https://doi.org/10. 1177/0886260514554290

Krieger, M. A. (2020). *Image-based sexual violence: Victim experiences and bystander responses* (Doctoral thesis). Department of Psychology, University of Windsor. Scholarship at UWindsor. https://scholar.uwindsor.ca/etd/8335

Kroshus, E. (2018). College athletes, pluralistic ignorance and bystander behaviors to prevent sexual assault. *Journal of Clinical Sport Psychology, 13*(2), 330–344. https://doi.org/10.1123/jcsp.2018-0039

Lamb, S., & Attwell, L. (2019). Bystanders in 'sketchy' sexual situations: Their constructions of the 'girl', the 'guy', and themselves. *Feminism & Psychology*, *29*(3), 391–408. https://doi.org/10.1177/0959353518821150

Lodge, J., & Frydenberg, E. (2005). The role of peer bystanders in school bullying: Positive steps toward promoting peaceful schools. *Theory into Practice*, *44*(4), 329–336.

Mainwaring, C. (2023). *An investigation into the role of individual, situational, and contextual facilitators and barriers of bystander intervention intent in image-based sexual abuse contexts* (Doctoral thesis). Goldsmiths, University of London. Goldsmiths Research Online. https://research.gold.ac.uk/id/epr int/33325/

Mainwaring, C., Gabbert, F., & Scott, A. J. (2023a). A systematic review exploring variables related to bystander intervention in sexual violence contexts. *Trauma, Violence & Abuse*, *24*(3), 1727–1742. https://doi.org/10.1177/15248380221079660

Mainwaring, C., Scott, A. J., & Gabbert, F. (2023b). Behavioral intentions of bystanders to image-based sexual abuse: A preliminary focus group study with a university student sample. *Journal of Child Sexual Abuse*, *32*(3), 318–339. https://doi.org/10.1080/10538712.2023.2190734

Mainwaring, C., Scott, A. J., & Gabbert, F. (2024). Facilitators and barriers of bystander intervention intent in image-based sexual abuse contexts: A focus group study with a university sample. *Journal of Interpersonal Violence*, *39*(11–12), 2655–2686. https://doi.org/10.1177/08862605231222452

McGlynn, C., Rackley, E., Johnson, K., Henry, N., Gavey, N., Flynn, A., & Powell, A. (2021). 'It's torture for the soul:' The harms of image-based sexual abuse. *Social & Legal Studies*, *30*(4), 541–562. https://doi.org/10.1177/0964663920947791

Mckinlay, T., & Lavis, T. (2020). Why did she send it in the first place? Victim-blame in the context of 'revenge porn.' *Psychiatry, Psychology and Law*, *27*(3), 386–396. https://doi.org/10.1080/13218719.2020.1734977

Office of the eSafety Commissioner. (2017). *Image-based abuse: National survey—Summary report*. Retrieved 21 October, 2024, from https://www.esafety.gov.au/about-us/research/image-based-abuse

Palmer, J. E., Nicksa, S. C., & McMahon, S. (2018). Does who you know affect how you act? The impact of relationships on bystander intervention in interpersonal violence situations. *Journal of Interpersonal Violence*, *33*(17), 2623–2642. https://doi.org/10.1177/0886260516628292

Pina, A., Bell, A., Griffin, K., & Vasquez, E. (2021). Image-based sexual abuse proclivity and victim-blaming: The role of dark personality traits and moral disengagement. *Oñati Socio-Legal Series*, *11*(5), 1179–1197.

Powell, A., Scott, A. J., Flynn, A., & Henry, N. (2020). *Image-based sexual abuse: An international study of victims and perpetrators*. RMIT University.

Retrieved October 21, 2024, from https://www.researchgate.net/public
ation/339488012_Image-based_sexual_abuse_An_international_study_of_v
ictims_and_perpetrators

Powell, A., Scott, A. J., Flynn, A., & McCook, S. (2022). A multi-country study
of image-based sexual abuse: Extent, relational nature and correlates of victimisation experiences. *Journal of Sexual Aggression, 30*(1), 25–40. https://doi.
org/10.1080/13552600.2022.2119292

Pugh, B., Ningard, H., Ven, T. V., & Butler, L. (2016). Victim ambiguity:
Bystander intervention and sexual assault in the college drinking scene.
Deviant Behavior, 37(4), 401–418. https://doi.org/10.1080/01639625.
2015.1026777

Wamboldt, A., Khan, S. R., Mellins, C. A., & Hirsch, J. S. (2019). Friends,
strangers, and bystanders: Informal practices of sexual assault intervention.
Global Public Health, 14(1), 53–64. https://doi.org/10.1080/17441692.
2018.1472290

Zvi, L., & Shechory Bitton, M. (2021). Perceptions of victim and offender culpability in non-consensual distribution of intimate images. *Psychology, Crime &
Law, 27*(5), 427–442. https://doi.org/10.1080/1068316X.2020.1818236

CHAPTER 5

The Role of Gender in Bystander Intervention

Abstract In the Image-Based Abuse and Bystander Intervention Study, gender was a consistent factor to emerge in discussions around bystander intervention and image-based sexual abuse. This was evident in relation to the level of blame placed on the victim-survivor for their experience (see Chapter 3), the motivations of the perpetrator, and whether participants felt they would intervene if witnessing a real or hypothetical image-based sexual abuse incident. In this chapter, we discuss in more detail how gender dynamics may impact bystander intervention in image-based sexual abuse incidents, particularly the gender of bystanders, perpetrators, and victim-survivors.

Keywords Image-based sexual abuse · Bystander · Intervention · Gender · Attitudes

INTRODUCTION

Broadly speaking, gender identity is a key factor that influences a person's perceived propensity to intervene when witnessing sexual violence. Much of the intervention literature has found that women are more likely than men to perceive that they would intervene when witnessing sexual

© The Author(s), under exclusive license to Springer Nature 107
Switzerland AG 2025
A. Flynn et al., *Image-Based Sexual Abuse and Bystander Intervention*,
Palgrave Studies in Cybercrime and Cybersecurity,
https://doi.org/10.1007/978-3-031-83647-3_5

violence, but that they may take less risky behaviour when intervening, such as supporting the victim-survivor (see Mainwaring et al., 2023). However, such gender differences do not tend to play out when examining actual bystander intervention (Mainwaring et al., 2023). There is much less research on whether the gender of the victim-survivor and perpetrator plays a role on either the likelihood or the type of intervention taken. In this chapter, we sought to test whether gender (of bystanders, perpetrators and victim-survivors) was a consideration in bystander intervention, and what role it may play in a person's willingness or capacity to intervene. Here, we report on how gender shaped participants' views, responses, and considerations in bystander intervention. We begin with a discussion of the survey data.

The Role of Gender: Survey

In the survey data, there were some notable differences in the four types of actions (confront the perpetrator, report the behaviour, support the victim-survivor, do something else) that participants perceived they would take when witnessing image-based sexual abuse according to perpetrator gender and victim-survivor gender (see Table 5.1).

Regarding perpetrator gender, participants were more likely to indicate that they would confront a female perpetrator (75.9%) than a male perpetrator (63.9%), and more likely to report the behaviour of a male

Table 5.1 Behavioural intentions, % (n)

	Confront the perpetrator (n = 184)	Report the behaviour (n = 184)	Support the victim-survivor (n = 184)	Something else (n = 184)
Perpetrator gender				
Female	75.9% (66)	9.2% (8)	11.5% (10)	11.5% (10)
Male	63.9% (62)	18.6% (18)	14.4% (14)	15.5% (15)
Overall	69.6 (128)	14.1% (26)	13.0% (24)	13.6% (25)
Victim-survivor gender				
Female	64.9% (61)	19.1% (18)	14.9% (14)	14.9% (14)
Male	74.4% (67)	8.9% (8)	11.1% (10)	12.2% (11)
Overall	69.6 (128)	14.1% (26)	13.0% (24)	13.6% (25)

Note All comparisons utilise the sample of participants who responded to the open-question regarding what they would say or do (*n* = 184)

perpetrator (18.6%) than a female perpetrator (9.2%). Regarding victim-survivor gender, participants were significantly more likely to report the behaviour when the victim-survivor was a woman (19.1%), rather than a man (8.9%).

When participants were asked whether their view of the situation would change if the perpetrator and/or victim-survivor was a man, instead of a woman, or vice versa, most participants believed they would 'definitely not' or 'probably not' change their view if the perpetrator's gender changed (M = 1.56), or if the victim-survivor's gender changed (M = 1.49) (see Table 5.2).

Regarding perpetrator gender, participants were more likely to believe their view would change when presented with the female perpetrator scenario and asked to imagine that the perpetrator was a man (M = 1.67), compared to when they were presented with the male perpetrator scenario and asked to imagine that the perpetrator was a woman (1.46). Regarding victim-survivor gender, participants were significantly more likely to believe their view would change when presented with the male victim-survivor scenario and asked to imagine that the victim-survivor was a woman (M = 1.61), compared to when they were presented with the female victim-survivor scenario and asked to imagine that the perpetrator was a man (M = 1.37). Although all averages fell within the 'definitely not' and 'probably not' range, participants were less definite in their beliefs when asked to imagine the perpetrator was a man, and the victim-survivor was a woman.

Table 5.2 What if the perpetrator's and victim-survivor's gender had been different, M (SD)

	Likelihood of viewing differently
Perpetrator gender	
Imagine perpetrator was a man	1.67 (1.09)
Imagine perpetrator was a woman	1.46 (0.94)
Overall	1.56 (1.02)
Victim-survivor gender	
Imagine victim-survivor was a man	1.37 (0.78)
Imagine victim-survivor was a woman	1.61 (1.01)
Overall	1.49 (0.91)

Note Measured via a 5-point scale ranging from '1 not at all' to '5 very much'

Perpetrator Gender

When survey participants believed their view would change if the perpetrator's gender was different, they tended to focus on men being more likely to engage in this type of behaviour, and the broader context of misogyny, power, and control. This is reflected in the following comments:

> It is still inappropriate, but there would definitely be a sense of justice or payback at heterosexual males as a collective for their treatment towards women in society. (P184 ADE M)

> Would be reflective of underlying misogyny and treatment of women in society. (P098 SYD F)

> When a man send[s] pictures without consent it is usually about power and control. (P170 MEL F)

In this sense, participants felt there was more of a need to intervene when the perpetrator was a man, despite the survey data showing participants were more likely to intervene when the perpetrator was a woman. In contrast, participants tended to focus on the sameness of the situation in both principal and reality, when they did not believe their view would change if the perpetrator's gender was different. As the following comments describe:

> No-one has the right to violate anyone's privacy no matter what gender they are. (P024 SYD F)

> Gender doesn't matter. (P053 ADE M)

> They're a person. Gender doesn't change their actions or its consequences. (P139 CAN M)

Similar views were expressed in the focus group scenarios, which we discuss later in this chapter.

Victim-Survivor Gender

When survey participants believed their view would change if the victim-survivor's gender was different, they tended to focus on the perceived vulnerability of women, and the increased stigma experienced by women compared to men when sexual imagery is shared without consent:

> It would have been worse. Women typically are more vulnerable in such positions and are more likely to face a bigger backlash or victim-survivor blaming from society as a result of such an event. As such I think I would tend to be more outraged if Sam [victim-survivor] was a woman. (P038 MEL F)

> Because women are perceived as more vulnerable. (P101 MEL F)

> I think there's a much higher level of stigma women experience when it comes to being sexual or leaked nudes/videos that men don't. If a man's nudes/sex video were to be made public there would be much less negative consequences for him I feel. The 'revenge' would have less impact on a man than a woman in my opinion. (P232 MEL M)

This sense of women as vulnerable was also a prominent theme to emerge in the focus group data, which we discuss in more detail later in this chapter, building on the discussion in Chapter 3. In contrast, participants tended to focus on the comparability of the situation and underlying principle when they did not believe their view would change if the victim-survivor's gender was different. As these comments suggest:

> It doesn't matter if it was a man or woman, friend or stranger, the fact that Taylor [perpetrator] didn't ask Sam's [victim-survivor's] permission was the biggest issue. (P023 MEL F)

> Consent applies equally to men and women. (P043 MEL F)

> The issue is about privacy and consent, not gender. (P102 CAN M)

The Role of Gender: Focus Groups

To further test if gender made a difference to bystander intervention, across the focus group scenarios we altered the gender of the perpetrator in both scenarios, and the gender of the victim-survivor in S1 (see Table 2.8 in Chapter 2 or Appendix Table A.1 for details of the scenarios). Overall, 18 focus groups had S1 with a male perpetrator and female victim-survivor, and S2 with a male perpetrator and transwoman victim-survivor; while 17 focus groups had S1 with a female perpetrator and male victim-survivor, and S2 with a female perpetrator and transwoman victim-survivor. Additionally, at the end of the discussion of each scenario, participants were asked whether any of their opinions would change if the gender of the perpetrator had been different. When explicitly asked this question, participants consistently stated that it would not change their response:

> Q: Would your reaction, whether you would or wouldn't intervene, do anything, be different if Lou [perpetrator] was a woman?
>
> M1: So, woman to woman?
>
> Q: Yes, so a woman is taking a photo of Alex [victim-survivor].
>
> F1: No.
>
> F2: No.
>
> M1: I don't think it's any different.
>
> F3: It's going to be the same.
>
> F4: Same. It should be the same. (FG5 ADE)

Similarly in another focus group (FG4 MEL):

> Q: Would you feel differently, or act differently, if Lou had been a woman taking the photo?
>
> F2: No.

M1: No, it's the same.

F1: Still creepy.

F3: Yes, wrong either way. It doesn't matter on your gender.

However, in the broader discussions of the hypothetical scenarios, gender was evidently a key barrier and facilitator of intervention. As a starting point, gender was a factor that influenced whether participants would feel comfortable or safe intervening, particularly where the focus group participant was a woman, and the perpetrator in S2 was a man. As one participant explained, 'if it was a man, I would not say a damn thing' (FG2 SYD F2). Others observed that 'you'd be more worried about Lou's [perpetrator] reaction if it was a man' (FG10 ADE F2), compared to 'if she's, like, a little woman, I wouldn't be so scared' (FG9 ADE F3). In one focus group (FG3 ADE), there was universal agreement among the female participants that if the perpetrator was a man, it would prevent them from saying or doing anything:

F1: I think, for women, I don't want to generalise here though, but there are different issues with physical safety.

F3: Yeah. We're more vulnerable, no matter what you say.

F1: I certainly carry with me a fear of confronting men, because being a woman in a public space, and trying to take up any kind of public space, and to challenge men, can be incredibly risky.

Some female participants who indicated that they would be prepared to intervene when Lou was a female perpetrator ultimately reflected that they would be less likely to do so if Lou was a man. As one observed, she would feel 'way more comfortable' (FG5 ADE F2) intervening if the perpetrator was a woman. Another female participant noted:

The fact that she's a 30-year-old woman might make you – and me as a female – you might feel a little bit more inclined to feel comfortable saying something. If it was a male then maybe like you [another participant] said, you don't if they're going to follow you. (FG7 ADE F2)

This was further demonstrated in the following excerpt from one of the focus groups (FG4 MEL):

F3: You'd feel – you'd be able to approach a female easier.

F1: Yeah, I feel like it would still be a bit more of a mouthy situation than a physical confrontation.

F6: It's less worrying.

F1: There's no, like, fear for safety, as such.

As noted in the excerpt above, changing one's preparedness to intervene because of the perpetrator's gender was primarily related to the ability of bystanders to maintain their personal safety and the social conditioning not to put oneself at risk with men. Similar views were shared in another focus group (FG3 CAN):

F1: It doesn't change my feelings about it, but going on that safety and confrontation sort of line, then I'm probably not going to say, 'excuse me'. I would definitely be trying to quickly think of other ways to do it.

F3: Yeah. … If there was a security person around, I would go to them rather than confront Lou [perpetrator] as a man, for safety [reasons].

This supports the results of research exploring bystander intervention in both offline and cyber bullying incidents, which reveal that bystanders react differently according to their own gender (Bastiaensens et al., 2014; Obermann, 2011; Oh & Hazler, 2009; Pöyhönen et al., 2012).

For the most part, male participants who were prepared to intervene said that they would do so regardless of whether Lou [perpetrator] was a man or a woman. However, several of the male participants said that if Lou was a woman, it would make them less likely to intervene or could alter the action that they would take. As these male participants reflected:

Can I add a gender thing there? I can imagine a woman wanting to defend the woman, I'd feel really awkward about saying, 'Do you know he just took a picture of you?' another bloke. I don't think that's going to work. She'd suddenly think, 'He's a bloke' … Why was he looking over? …

Woman to woman is far more likely to be accepted. I don't think she'd want to hear from me. (FG6 ADE M2)

If it's a woman taking a photograph of another woman, I wouldn't intervene. (FG5 ADE M5)

I really don't think I would step in there. If it looked like it was a more aggressive dude taking a photo of a woman, I would be more concerned. But, like, two chicks, I'm, like, do whatever. (FG7 SYD M2)

This shift in relation to intervention reflects two main gendered assumptions. The first is that it would be more challenging for a man to intervene effectively if the act was committed by a woman. This appeared to be based on a lack of confidence in having the appropriate skills to intervene and a perception that it wasn't a man's place to intervene. Further, some male participants reflected that they would feel more confident if a confrontation were to turn physical with another man, rather than if the perpetrator was a woman. As these two male participants discussed in one focus group (FG9 ADE):

M3: I would feel more confident confronting a guy, personally, because I know I can – I feel more confident being physical, if it came to that.

M2: I feel like if it was a male and depending on their stature and how many people are around, I would feel more obliged to call them out on it straight away and be really confrontational in that regard ... but yeah, I wouldn't be – weirdly I don't think I'd be able to confront a woman about it in a weird way, perhaps because I don't know the appropriate way to confront somebody.

The second gendered assumption was a disbelief among some participants that this type of offending behaviour would be committed by a woman, against another woman, leading to a sense of ambiguity around the nature of the incident. As the following excerpts highlight, these views were due to gendered assumptions about who perpetrates and who experiences sexual violence:

I'd be shocked, probably, because I would just not think it would be [done by a woman]. It's a thing that creepy men do. ... That would be really strange if it was a case of that, and I just do not like to think about it [a woman committing that act]. (FG3 CAN M1)

I would be totally thrown if, I mean, I would be thrown anyway if I saw that happen, but I would be totally thrown if I saw a woman doing that. Yeah, I think, even more so if it was a woman I'd be like, 'What kinky town have we stopped off here?'. (FG10 MEL F1)

It's a woman? That's the other thing that I was shocked at, that it was actually a female taking photographs. I'm used to men [doing this], but not women. (FG8 SYD F4)

Although statistically speaking men are more likely to perpetrate sexual violence compared to women (Doherty & Dowling, 2024), these perspectives are concerning as they may serve to minimise the experiences of victim-survivors where the perpetrator is a woman.

Participants commonly relied on their own normalised gendered assumptions around how women should behave, how women should interact with each other, and the motivations as to why women would engage in this behaviour as both hindering them, and encouraging them, to intervene. For example, participants expressed a greater sense of sadness (for the victim-survivor), and some even felt more offended by the behaviour when it involved a female perpetrator:

I actually think I would be way more upset. I would feel that Lou [perpetrator] should have a better understanding of the way that, in this case, like her actions would impact Alex [victim-survivor]. And I would be like, 'You are a woman. You should understand this'. (FG2 ADE M2)

It's a weird situation. Again, I guess because it's a woman I'd feel more personally affronted. (FG5 ADE F2)

As discussed in Chapter 3 in relation to the perceived gendered motivations of the male versus female perpetrator in S1, participants also applied gendered assumptions to the perpetrator's behaviour in S2. This included changing the motivation for the behaviour from being sexual, to instead about bullying—assuming that women would not sexualise other women—and changing the way they perceived the nature of the relationship between the perpetrator and victim-survivor to assume there must be some kind of existing relationship for this exchange to happen—assuming a woman would not engage in this behaviour with a stranger:

> I think if she was a female, it could be more sort of like, bully ... Yeah, a bullying case. So, the nature could be different. (FG9 MEL M3)

> I think I would just assume they were friends, that if I did get involved in some way, that they'd be like, this is none of your business, they're more likely to say that [because they are women]. (FG6 MEL F2)

One focus group discussion also led to a perception that when the woman was the perpetrator, she must have been under the control or direction of her male partner—'she might be being paid by her male partner' (FG5 ADE F2).

One group (FG1 MEL) also reflected on how the gender of the perpetrator might affect the support you would receive from other bystanders when intervening. Given that participants expressed their own conflicting attitudes towards the behaviour if it was perpetrated by a woman, they similarly believed that they may receive less support from other bystanders if this was the case:

> M1: I feel you'd get more support if there were people on the train, if it was a male taking a photo of a female.

> M2: Yeah.

> M1: You know, asking for that help from bystanders or eyeballing people, I think you'd get a lot more support if it was a male taking the picture of a female.

> M2: Yeah, correct.

Gender was also a barrier to intervention in S1; however, this was connected to both the gender composition of the group of friends and the gender identity of the perpetrator. In this instance, participants perceived they may be less likely to intervene among a group of male friends. As one participant reflected:

I think it would depend on who the group is. If it was a group of female friends, you might be a little bit more inclined to pipe up and say something. Whereas if it's a bunch of guys going, 'Ha ha, look at this!', you feel a bit awkward. (FG7 ADE F2)

A similar reflection was provided by one of the male participants, who stated that if it was a group of male friends, he would be less likely to intervene:

It really depends on the group. Like, I know for myself, if it's a group of really kind of like alpha males, I would definitely not say anything because I myself would feel threatened. It really does depend on the group. (FG9 ADE M1)

The perceived difference in how male versus female friends would react to being shown a non-consensual nude image was a strong theme to emerge across all focus groups. The following exchanges show how female participants felt that a group of male friends might perceive them to be over-reacting if they did intervene primarily because of their gender:

If it had been a group of mostly male friends and I'd been there, you run the risk of them going, if it's all guys and you're the only girl, and you say something, you could be getting a bit of backlash about, you're a woman, stop being so sensitive. (FG6 MEL F5)

I think if it was all men, there's that sense of, 'Can't you take a joke?', that kind of thing that men sometimes give women when they have an issue with sexist behaviour. It's like, 'We're just kidding. Lighten up'. So, I think if it was more men, I'd probably feel a bit less confident [to intervene] than if it was all women. (FG6 SYD F2)

These comments highlight the key role that gender can play in shaping bystander responses and their willingness to intervene. In the next section, we explore how gender identity expands beyond the male/female binary to also influence if and how bystanders may approach intervention in image-based sexual abuse incidents.

ALEX'S GENDER IDENTITY

In S2, the victim-survivor's gender identity as a transwoman was acknowledged as being a factor that would influence participants' actions and willingness to intervene. Some focus group participants felt they would be more likely to confront the perpetrator because they recognised the challenges and discrimination experienced by transwomen. As the following participants described:

> I'd do something. My instinct would be to give a loud dressing down of his behaviour, because it's fucking disgusting, and particularly just the dynamics of the genders and stuff, and all the oppression against transwomen in particular would just make me think, that is so not on. You'd try to intervene in that situation to stop him doing that immediately, without much other thought going into it. (FG3 CAN M1)

> Particularly being transgender too, because they cop enough harassment, enough stigma, enough everything – that's so completely inappropriate. If I saw anything like that, I'd call it out. ... It's just wrong. (FG1 SYD M1)

There was also a common concern raised around the motivation for this abuse being fuelled by discrimination towards transgender people. One participant commented: 'I think another part of the issue is that she is transgender. So, knowing a lot of people who are trans who have experienced a lot of this stuff, it's not so much just sexual, it's also pointing out that someone is different'. (FG4 SYD F2)

For other participants, the marginalisation and discrimination Alex [victim-survivor] may have experienced previously was a reason not to intervene or to tell her what had happened. As one participant described:

> The thing is, I'm reading that Alex is a transwoman. As a member of that community, as a minority, I feel like she already experiences – or would be struggling enough. So, I would want to spare her that extra burden [of telling her it happened]. (FG3 SYD F2)

For others, the potential history of discrimination meant they would change how they would intervene. For example, rather than making a public scene, they would be more inclined to intervene by quietly telling Alex, which they perceived would give her autonomy over how the situation was then handled:

A transperson can already feel incredibly visible and may not want to be seen in the way of you yelling that this creeper is taking a photo of them. So, I might try to get to them first, and just say, because it's great being an ally, but it's not always the case that other people want you to speak for them. So, to just say, I have observed this, would you like me to do anything? I will do something. I will do what you want though. Because … you have no idea, you don't know what they might want done. (FG3 ADE F1)

You might not want to create a bigger scene. It's up to Alex, because it's quite humiliating already, and being a transwoman would be difficult anyway. So, I don't know, she might not necessarily want more attention drawn to her. (FG8 MEL F2)

Although the presence of other bystanders was, generally speaking, seen as a facilitator for action in relation to S2, participants also reflected on how some members of the public may not be supportive because of potential discriminatory attitudes towards transgender people, and this would then impact whether and how they would intervene:

I'd definitely tell Alex, I'm not sure I would confront Lou [perpetrator] because I just have to consider the power dynamics here because transwomen are at a disproportionate likelihood to receive violence, and you can't always count on the fact that people in public will be on her side. (FG7 MEL F1)

Especially like given that she's a transwoman, she's going to feel more attacked. Her safety is going to be at a higher degree of risk. (FG2 SYD F2)

Alex's gender identity was also recognised as a key reason why participants would not contact the police, or encourage Alex to contact the police, unless she specifically chose to take that option herself. Several participants (as reflected by the following comment) noted that they would 'definitely go with Alex to the police, because sending a transwoman alone to the police is potentially dangerous' (FG10 MEL M1). Others expanded on this view, stating that 'police can be pretty violent against transpeople and wouldn't necessarily believe her. … The police might be more likely to harass her' (FG10 SYD M2). Other participants commented on this potential discrimination, stating:

I would not tell a police officer or a ticket inspector or something, but that's mainly based on my opinion about them being awful people that abuse lots of minorities, in particular, transpeople. So, I would think that getting them involved wouldn't be something I would be [up] for. I think the decision's up to Alex, but it wouldn't be something that I would jump to do. (FG3 CAN M1)

These comments are reflective of much of the literature on transpeople's experiences with police (Alliance for a Safe & Diverse DC, 2008; Berman & Robinson, 2010; Grant et al., 2011; Israel et al., 2013; Miles-Johnson, 2016). For example, Langenderfer-Magruder et al. (2016) found that transgender people were significantly less likely to report experiences of intimate partner violence to the police than cisgender persons, due to doubt that they would be treated fairly or taken seriously. Fear and mistrust of the police have also been identified as key factors that impact transpeople and gender-diverse people's likelihood to report to the police (Campbell & Raja, 1999; Silver & Miller, 2004). Serpe and Nadal's (2017) study of 266 participants ($n = 66$ cisgender male, $n = 147$ cisgender female, $n = 53$ transgender) found that transgender people reported less comfort interacting with the police, higher levels of police victimisation, discrimination and bias, and higher negative perceptions of police than cisgender men and cisgender women. As a result, transgender participants were less likely to interact with the police.

Overall, the normalised gendered assumptions, and the gender identity of the bystanders, perpetrators, and victim-survivors present were clear factors influencing bystander intervention across the focus groups, and provide an interesting consideration for both future research and for the development of educational or other resources to ensure that gender is included as a key focus.

CONCLUSION

This chapter has presented a discussion on some of the ways in which gender impacts on bystander attitudes and actions. Similar to the discussion in Chapter 3, we found gender to be a significant factor that impacts on bystander intervention—in ways both acknowledged and unacknowledged by participants. This chapter has provided insight into the various ways that gender dynamics, assumptions, and myths may contribute to action and inaction on the part of bystanders, demonstrating the role that gender plays in bystander intervention and image-based sexual abuse.

REFERENCES

Alliance for a Safe & Diverse DC. (2008). *Move along: Policing sex work in Washington, D.C.—A report by the Alliance for a Safe & Diverse DC.* Retrieved October 21, 2024, from https://dctranscoalition.wordpress.com/wp-content/uploads/2010/05/movealongreport.pdf

Berman, A., & Robinson, S. (2010). *Speaking out: Stopping homophobic and transphobic abuse in Queensland.* Australian Academic Press.

Campbell, R., & Raja, S. (1999). Secondary victimization of rape victims: Insights from mental health professionals who treat survivors of violence. *Violence and Victims, 14*(3), 261–275. https://doi.org/10.1891/0886-6708.14.3.261

Doherty, L., & Dowling, C. (2024). *Perpetration of sexual violence in a community sample of adult Australians.* Statistical Bulletin no. 45. Australian Institute of Criminology. https://doi.org/10.52922/sb77352

Grant, J. M., Mottet, L. A., Tanis, J., Harrison, J., Herman, J. L., & Keisling, M. (2011). *Injustice at every turn: A report of the National Transgender Discrimination Survey.* Retrieved October 21, 2024, from https://transequality.org/sites/default/files/docs/resources/NTDS_Report.pdf

Israel, T., Harkness, A., Delucio, K., Ledbetter, J. N., & Avellar, T. R. (2013). Evaluation of police training on LGBTQ issues: Knowledge, interpersonal apprehension, and self-efficacy. *Journal of Police and Criminal Psychology, 29*(2), 1–11. https://doi.org/10.1007/s11896-013-9132-z

Langenderfer-Magruder, L., Whitfield, D. L., Walls, N. E., Kattari, S. K., & Ramos, D. (2016). Experiences of intimate partner violence and subsequent police reporting among lesbian, gay, bisexual, transgender, and queer adults in Colorado: Comparing rates of cisgender and transgender victimization. *Journal of Interpersonal Violence, 31*(5), 855–871. https://doi.org/10.1177/0886260514556767

Mainwaring, C., Gabbert, F., & Scott, A. J. (2023). A systematic review exploring variables related to bystander intervention in sexual violence contexts. *Trauma, Violence, & Abuse, 24*(3), 1727–1742. https://doi.org/10.1177/15248380221079660

Miles-Johnson, T. (2016). Policing diversity: Examining police resistance to training reforms for transgender people in Australia. *Journal of Homosexuality, 63*(1), 103–106. https://doi.org/10.1080/00918369.2015.1078627

Serpe, C. R., & Nadal, K. L. (2017). Perceptions of police: Experience in the trans* community. *Journal of Gay & Lesbian Social Services, 29*(3), 280–299. https://doi.org/10.1080/10538720.2017.1319777

Silver, E., & Miller, L. L. (2004). Sources of informal social control in Chicago neighborhoods. *Criminology, 42*(3), 551–583. https://doi.org/10.1111/j.1745-9125.2004.tb00529.x

CHAPTER 6

Bystanders and Image-Based Sexual Abuse: A Conclusion

Abstract This final chapter brings together the key findings from the Image-Based Sexual Abuse and Bystander Study. It shines light on the new and ongoing challenges surrounding the prevention of image-based sexual abuse and reflects on the importance of empowering bystanders to take positive action in response to image-based sexual abuse. It also outlines limitations of the study, and proposes a future research agenda for scholars, researchers, and students working in this area.

Keywords Image-based sexual abuse · Bystander · Intervention

INTRODUCTION

Given the limited knowledge base, there has been an urgent need for research to explore the factors that influence bystander intervention in image-based sexual abuse contexts. The Image-Based Sexual Abuse and Bystander Study sought to build on, and fill gaps in, existing knowledge of bystander intervention to examine attitudes towards, and awareness of, image-based sexual abuse, applicable laws, and available options to respond to, or counter, such behaviours. Specifically, we focused on

A. Flynn et al., *Image-Based Sexual Abuse and Bystander Intervention*, Palgrave Studies in Cybercrime and Cybersecurity, https://doi.org/10.1007/978-3-031-83647-3_6

123

people's willingness or preparedness to intervene, and the barriers and facilitators to bystander action. The two main aims of the study were to:

1. Understand bystander attitudes towards image-based sexual abuse, and measure their capacity and willingness to intervene when witnessing these behaviours, and
2. Identify the key influencing factors for bystanders, including the barriers and facilitators to intervention, when they witness image-based sexual abuse.

To address these aims, we conducted an online, anonymous survey with 245 Australian residents (aged 18–71 years) and 35 in-person focus groups with 219 participants across Australia. In this final chapter, we bring together three overarching findings from the study: attitudes and victim-blaming; barriers and facilitators to bystander intervention; and the role of gender in bystander intervention. We also outline limitations of the study and areas for future research.

ATTITUDES AND VICTIM-BLAMING

The survey data produced concerning findings around men's willingness and capacity to intervene when witnessing image-based sexual abuse incidents, including their greater propensity to attribute blame to victim-survivors, to minimise the harms of image-based sexual abuse, and to express concerns about whether intervention will impact their relationship with the perpetrator. This corresponds with previous research on bystander intervention showing that men are more likely to be accepting of myths surrounding sexual violence, and to be concerned about their relationship with the perpetrator, which can act as key barriers to intervention (Banyard, 2008; Banyard et al., 2007), or can influence the type of intervention that men choose to undertake (Kaya et al., 2019; Wamboldt et al., 2019). It also supports research on image-based sexual abuse, which has found that men are more likely than women to blame victim-survivors and to minimise the harms of image-based sexual abuse (Attrill-Smith et al., 2021; Bothamley & Tully, 2018; Flynn et al., 2023, 2024a; Henry et al., 2019; Scott & Gavin, 2018; Zvi & Bitton, 2020). Overall, we found that men and heterosexual individuals are more likely to blame victim-survivors of image-based sexual abuse if they have previously taken or shared intimate images of themselves, and to believe that intimate image sharing is acceptable in certain situations (e.g. when the images were not wanted or asked for). This finding may be partially due to the gendered and heteronormative dynamics that shape perceptions of risk, blame, and responsibility in sexual image sharing (Flynn et al., 2023). Another potential explanation is that the consensual sharing of nude or sexual images is more common and normalised among LGBQI+ people (Comunello et al., 2021; Flynn et al., 2024b; Van Ouytsel et al., 2020a, 2020b), thereby reducing some of the stigma associated with intimate image sharing (Paradiso et al., 2024).

Victim-blaming rhetoric was also present in the 'what if' questions in the survey, and within the focus groups, with participants commenting that people lose control over intimate images that they send to others, and thus are partially responsible if their images are subsequently shared. In the hypothetical scenarios presented in the focus groups, the 'wrongness' of the perpetrator's behaviour in non-consensually sharing sexual imagery was perceived by participants to be somewhat reduced when the victim-survivor was involved in the initial creation of the imagery, as in S1 (see Table 2.8 in Chapter 2 or Appendix Table A.1 for details of the scenarios). Although participants shied away from using the term 'blame', some still described the victim-survivor's actions in sending the image as being 'risky' and therefore opening them up to this form of abuse. The clear absence of consent in S2 resulted in less blame or responsibility being attributed to the victim-survivor by the focus group participants, with the overwhelming majority attributing no blame in this scenario. However, some participants still perceived that the clothing choice of the victim-survivor—described as 'a skirt'—might attract unwanted attention and suggested that they would tell the victim-survivor to be more conscious about their state of dress. This is reminiscent of victim-blaming rhetoric that centres on what victim-survivors were wearing at the time of the abuse (see Burgin & Flynn, 2021; Flynn, 2015).

It was positive that overall perceptions of blame in the survey responses were low, and that there were few victim-blaming comments shared during the focus groups, yet it is possible that the latter is because participants were not comfortable expressing such beliefs in a group setting. Narratives of victim-blame and shame are highly problematic, as they place responsibility on victim-survivors to prevent sexual violence from occurring, rather than on perpetrators. These attitudes also have important implications for bystander behaviour. In the context of bystander intervention, challenging victim-blaming attitudes can help ensure that the reactions of other bystanders do not normalise or support abusive behaviour, thereby dissuading intervention (Voelpel et al., 2008).

Our survey findings also suggest that men are more likely to believe people can boost their reputation by sharing intimate images and to believe that people feel turned-on by having their images shared. Similar gendered perceptions around motivations and harms emerged in the focus groups, particularly in S1, where participants reflected more negatively on the behaviour of the person for sending the image initially when the participant was a man, as opposed to a woman, assuming that the behaviour was somehow motivated by sexual gratification, boosting their reputation, or as a form of sexual harassment. These findings are consistent with the small number of studies that have explored attitudes towards image-based sexual abuse, where participants perceive a situation with a female victim-survivor and male perpetrator as more serious than when the genders are reversed (Bothamley & Tully, 2018; Hudson et al., 2014; Pina et al., 2017; Scott & Gavin, 2018).

Barriers and Facilitators to Bystander Intervention

The survey and focus group findings support prior research indicating that many people do not intervene when witnessing image-based sexual abuse (e.g. see Office of the eSafety Commissioner, 2017; Powell et al., 2020). In our survey, 64.1% of participants had witnessed non-consensual imagery, but only 45.6% of these participants reported saying or doing something in response. A range of barriers and facilitators to intervention were identified. Primarily, these related to the nature of the relationship between all parties (bystander, victim-survivor, perpetrator, and other people present); the perceived risk of intervening (social implications or risk to safety); the gender of the bystander, the victim-survivor, and the perpetrator; and the perceived likelihood of receiving support from other bystanders. Perceptions of whether bystanders would receive support from others if they intervened are particularly important, given that previous research has identified that people often perceive that their peers will be less supportive than they actually are (Brown & Messman-Moore, 2010; Fabiano et al., 2003; Kroshus, 2018).

In S1, perceptions of risk centred around the social implications of intervention, such as the reactions of both the perpetrator and the broader social group, and highlighted the importance bystanders place on the nature of their relationship with the perpetrator and their peers. This somewhat reflects Darley and Latané's (1968) bystander effect theory (social influence). Perceptions of how others would respond influenced participants' decisions as to whether or not to intervene, aligning with Burn's (2009) 'evaluation apprehension' concept, whereby concerns that others will view intervention as unnecessary or inappropriate may hinder bystander intervention. In S2, the participants primarily focused on the potential risks to personal or physical safety posed by intervening, building on much of the existing research on bystander intervention (Fischer et al., 2011; Hamby et al., 2016; Lodge & Frydenberg, 2005).

One of the further factors we explored was whether beliefs regarding image-based sexual abuse laws would influence participants' likelihood to intervene. Despite the existence of image-based sexual abuse laws in each of the four locations in which the study took place (Adelaide, Canberra, Melbourne, and Sydney), participants demonstrated limited knowledge of the laws, particularly in relation to threatening to share non-consensual imagery. For example, while 66.1% of survey participants believed that it is a crime to upload an intimate image onto a website, only 38.8% believed that it is a crime to threaten to share an intimate image. The majority of these participants believed that image-based sexual abuse should 'probably' or 'definitely' be a crime.

Focus group participants had mixed perceptions around whether the scenarios presented to them depicted illegal behaviours. For S1, the murky nature of consent and the fact that the image was shown in person rather than distributed digitally resulted in some participants holding the view that the behaviour represented a lower-level harm that should not be criminalised. The belief that this form of image-based sexual abuse perpetration did not warrant criminalisation was linked to minimisation and normalisation of the sharing of intimate images more broadly. Participants identified challenges in collecting evidence and proving that a crime had occurred, particularly in circumstances where an image was shared in person rather than distributed. They also believed that the level of harm experienced by the victim-survivor should play a role in determining whether the behaviour was an offence. S2 produced much higher levels of agreement with statements supporting criminalisation, due to the clearer absence of consent, with most participants believing that the behaviour was, and should be, a crime. However, participants had concerns over the effectiveness of the police in responding to this behaviour and treating upskirting seriously.

Participants' perceptions and beliefs about the laws surrounding image-based sexual abuse did not appear to influence their likelihood of intervening when witnessing image-based sexual abuse. When discussing S1, almost no participants suggested involving the police, and most felt that if they did intervene, they would talk to the perpetrator, tell the victim-survivor, or stop hanging around with the perpetrator. In S2, participants agreed that the act of upskirting was an offence, but when discussing whether this would impact their likelihood to intervene in the matter, or what action they would take, the behaviour being illegal was not a dominant factor for bystander intervention. Instead, participants tended to focus on the potential harm to the victim-survivor. This finding suggests that educating the public about the laws surrounding image-based sexual abuse alone is insufficient to promote positive bystander intervention in cases of image-based sexual abuse. Thus, there is a need to explore other factors that may empower bystanders to intervene when witnessing these behaviours.

Overall, these findings further highlight the importance of having alternate avenues of support and justice available for victim-survivors of image-based sexual abuse, which are not solely reliant on criminal law. While the law plays an important role in highlighting image-based sexual abuse as a socially unacceptable behaviour, legal responses should be combined with non-legal options and education and prevention messaging (Flynn & Henry, 2021; Henry et al., 2019).

THE ROLE OF GENDER IN BYSTANDER INTERVENTION

Gender was a consistent factor to arise in discussions around bystander intervention and image-based sexual abuse. This was evident in the level of blame placed on the victim-survivor for their experience, the motivations of the perpetrator, and whether participants believed they would intervene if witnessing a real or hypothetical image-based sexual abuse incident. As a starting point, gender influenced whether participants would feel comfortable or safe intervening, particularly where the focus group participant was a woman, and the perpetrator was a man. In S2, many female participants who were prepared to intervene when the perpetrator was a woman, ultimately said that they would be less likely to do so if the perpetrator was a man. There were also differences in willingness to intervene by male participants, who felt that they would be less likely to do so if the perpetrator in S2 was a woman. This shift reflects two main gendered assumptions. The first relates to men finding it more challenging to intervene effectively with a female perpetrator, because they lack either confidence or knowledge of the appropriate skills to intervene, and that they perceived that intervention in this instance would be most effective through physical acts, which they were less prepared to do if the perpetrator was a woman. Second, there was disbelief that this type of offending behaviour would be committed by a woman, against another woman, which created some ambiguity around the nature of the incident. In this sense, participants' gendered assumptions around how women should behave, how women should interact with each other, and the motivations as to why women would engage in image-based sexual abuse behaviours both hindered and encouraged them to intervene.

Participants also applied gendered assumptions to the perpetrator's behaviour in S2. This included changing the motivation for the behaviour from sexual gratification to bullying, and changing the way they perceived the nature of the relationship between the perpetrator and victim-survivor to assume there must be some kind of existing relationship for this exchange to happen. Furthermore, some participants expressed a greater sense of sadness and felt more offended by the behaviour when it was perpetrated by a woman, because it was less socially expected of them, compared to men.

In S2, the victim-survivor's gender identity as a transwoman was identified as an influencing factor that would change participants' actions and willingness to intervene. Some participants felt they would be more likely to confront the perpetrator because of the challenges and discrimination experienced by transwomen. Others felt this was a reason not to intervene or to tell the victim-survivor. The victim-survivor's gender identity was also a key reason why participants would not contact the police or encourage the victim-survivor to contact the police, because they were concerned about how the police might treat the victim-survivor. Participants believed the police might be biased or discriminatory against transgender people, supporting the findings of other research in this space (Alliance for a Safe & Diverse DC, 2008; Berman & Robinson, 2010; Grant et al., 2011; Israel et al., 2013; Miles-Johnson, 2016). This finding is reflective of the experiences of transgender people with the police and the criminal justice system, including reduced likelihood of reporting to police due to concerns they will not be treated fairly or taken seriously (Bornstein et al., 2006; Grant et al., 2011; Langenderfer-Magruder et al., 2016), and due to fear and mistrust towards the police (Campbell & Raja, 1999; Silver & Miller, 2004). Overall, the normalised gendered assumptions and the gender identity of the bystander, perpetrator, victim-survivor, and other bystanders were dominant factors influencing bystander intervention in the study.

STUDY LIMITATIONS AND CONCLUSION

Like all research, this study has limitations. The research includes a non-probability sample of participants, which cannot claim to be representative of the Australian context or beyond. We also had more female than male participants, and only 11 participants specifically identified as non-binary, transgender, or other gender identity. This small sample meant that this cohort could not be included in the statistical analysis, although where possible we have included qualitative data from gender-diverse partic-ipants from the survey. This should be considered a limitation of the recruitment strategy and/or research findings and, given the findings in this research on gender identity and its role in bystander intervention, highlights the need for future research that engages with non-binary, transgender, or other gender identity communities to ensure a broader diversity of voices and experiences can be included in future research. In addition, the survey and focus group findings explored participants' perceptions regarding their likelihood of intervening when witnessing hypothetical scenarios of image-based sexual abuse. Therefore, it is impor-tant to recognise that people's perceptions may differ from whether and how they would intervene when confronted with a 'real-life' image-based sexual abuse incident. The potential for difference is evident in the litera-ture, which demonstrates that for the most part, women are more likely to perceive that they would intervene than men in sexual violence contexts, but that these gender differences are not borne out in actual interven-tion behaviour (Mainwaring et al., 2023). Despite the limitations, this is the first known mixed methods study of bystander intervention in image-based sexual abuse incidents and presents important insights.

This book provides new knowledge of bystander intervention and image-based sexual abuse, including barriers, facilitators, and the role of gender and laws in influencing people's willingness to intervene, but further research is needed. We suggest that future research be conducted with an intersectional gendered lens that explores additional power dynamics and factors, with a diversity of participants. There is also a need to further explore the development of educational materials to assist bystanders in safely intervening in instances of image-based sexual abuse. Research has consistently shown that education and awareness-raising are important in addressing and preventing abusive behaviours (Albury & Crawford, 2012; Campbell & Manganello, 2008; Carmody & Carrington, 2000; Döring, 2014; Gilliam et al., 2016; Schewe, 2007). However, the findings from the current study indicate that extending this education to improving knowledge of image-based sexual abuse laws may be ineffective in promoting positive bystander intervention. Previous research suggests that bystander messaging should outline ways to safely intervene (e.g. saying or doing something to the perpetrator, supporting the victim-survivor, and engaging the support of other bystanders), direct blame away from the victim-survivor towards the perpetrator, and shift responsibility to avoid, diffuse, or control the situation towards bystanders (Flynn et al., 2022a). It is apparent that further research is needed to explore other strategies that might be effective in empowering bystanders to intervene when witnessing image-based sexual abuse.

Image-based sexual abuse is a serious and significant social, legal, and public health problem that requires a multifaceted response. This is particularly important as new forms of image-based sexual abuse, such as sexualised deepfake abuse, are continuing to emerge (Flynn et al., 2022b, 2022c). Bystanders are one largely untapped resource that can contribute to disrupting and preventing image-based sexual abuse behaviours and help condone attitudes that blame the victim-survivor or minimise its harms. This book has provided insight into the new and ongoing challenges surrounding the prevention of image-based sexual abuse, and the importance of empowering bystanders to take positive action in response to image-based sexual abuse.

References

Albury, K., & Crawford, K. (2012). Sexting, consent and young people's ethics: Beyond Megan's story. *Continuum Journal of Media & Cultural Studies*, *26*(3), 463–473. https://doi.org/10.1080/10304312.2012.665840

Alliance for a Safe & Diverse DC. (2008). *Move along: Policing sex work in Washington, D.C.—A report by the Alliance for a Safe & Diverse DC.* Retrieved October 21, 2024, from https://dctranscoalition.wordpress.com/wp-content/uploads/2010/05/movealongreport.pdf

Attrill-Smith, A., Wesson, C. J., Chater, M. L., & Weekes, L. (2021). Gender differences in videoed accounts of victim blaming for revenge porn for self-taken and stealth-taken sexually explicit images and videos. *Cyberpsychology: Journal of Psychosocial Research on Cyberspace, 15*(4), Article 3. https://doi.org/10.5817/CP2021-4-3

Banyard, V. L. (2008). Measurement and correlates of prosocial bystander behavior: The case of interpersonal violence. *Violence and Victims, 23*(1), 83–97. https://doi.org/10.1891/0886-6708.23.1.83

Banyard, V. L., Moynihan, M. M., & Plante, E. G. (2007). Sexual violence prevention through bystander education: An experimental evaluation. *Journal of Community Psychology, 35*(4), 463–481. https://or.g/1002/jcop.20159

Berman, A., & Robinson, S. (2010). *Speaking out: Stopping homophobic and transphobic abuse in Queensland*. Australian Academic Press.

Bornstein, D. R., Fawcett, J., Sullivan, M., Senturia, K. D., & Shiu-Thornton, S. (2006). Understanding the experiences of lesbian, bisexual and trans survivors of domestic violence: A qualitative study. *Journal of Homosexuality, 51*(1), 159–181.

Bothamley, S., & Tully, R. J. (2018). Understanding revenge pornography: Public perceptions of revenge pornography and victim-blaming. *Journal of Aggression, Conflict and Peace Research, 10*(1), 1–10. https://doi.org/10.1108/JACPR-09-2016-0253

Burgin, R., & Flynn, A. (2021). Women's behavior as implied consent: Male "reasonableness" in Australian rape law. *Criminology & Criminal Justice, 21*(3), 334–352. https://doi.org/10.1177/1748895819880953

Brown, A. L., & Messman-Moore, T. L. (2010). Personal and perceived peer attitudes supporting sexual aggression as predictors of male college students' willingness to intervene against sexual aggression. *Journal of Interpersonal Violence, 25*(3), 503–517. https://doi.org/10.1177/0886260509334400

Burn, S. M. (2009). A situational model of sexual assault prevention through bystander intervention. *Sex Roles: A Journal of Research, 60*(11–12), 779–792. https://doi.org/10.1007/s11199-008-9581-5

Campbell, J. C., & Manganello, J. (2008). Changing public attitudes as a prevention to reduce intimate partner violence. *Journal of Aggression, Maltreatment & Trauma, 13*(3–4), 13–39. https://doi.org/10.1300/J146v13n03_02

Campbell, R., & Raja, S. (1999). Secondary victimization of rape victims: Insights from mental health professionals who treat survivors of violence. *Violence and Victims, 14*(3), 261–275. https://doi.org/10.1891/0886-6708.14.3.261

Carmody, M., & Carrington, K. (2000). Preventing sexual violence? *Australian and New Zealand Journal of Criminology, 33*(3), 341–361. https://doi.org/10.1177/000486580003300306

Comunello, F., Parisi, L., & Ieracitano, F. (2021). Negotiating gender scripts in mobile dating apps: Between affordances, usage norms and practices. *Information, Communication & Society, 24*(8), 1140–1156. https://doi.org/10.1080/1369118X.2020.1787485

Darley, J. M., & Latané, B. (1968). Bystander intervention in emergencies: Diffusion of responsibility. *Journal of Personality and Social Psychology, 8*(4, Pt. 1), 377–383. https://doi.org/10.1037/h0025589

Döring, N. (2014). Consensual sexting among adolescents: Risk prevention through abstinence education or safer sexting? *Cyberpsychology: Journal of Psychosocial Research on Cyberspace, 8*(1), Article 9. https://doi.org/10.5817/CP2014-1-9

Fabiano, P. M., Perkins, H. W., Berkowitz, A., Linkenbach, J., & Stark, C. (2003). Engaging men as social justice allies in ending violence against women: Evidence for a social norms approach. *Journal of American College Health, 52*(3), 105–112. https://doi.org/10.1080/07448030959573

Fischer, P., Krueger, J., Greitemeyer, T., Vogrincic, C., Kastenmüller, A., Frey, D., Heene, M., Wicher, M., & Kainbacher, M. (2011). The bystander-effect: A meta-analytic review on bystander intervention in dangerous and non-dangerous emergencies. *Psychological Bulletin, 137*(4), 517–537. https://doi.org/10.1037/a0023304

Flynn, A. (2015). Sexual violence and innovative responses to justice: Interrupting the recognisable narratives. In A. Powell, N. Henry, & A. Flynn (Eds.), *Rape justice: Beyond the criminal law* (pp. 92–111). Palgrave Macmillan.

Flynn, A., Cama, E., Powell, A., & Scott, A. J. (2023). Victim-blaming and image-based sexual abuse. *Journal of Criminology, 56*(1), 7–15. https://doi.org/10.1177/26338076221135327

Flynn, A., Cama, E., & Scott, A. J. (2022a). *Preventing image-based abuse in Australia: The role of bystanders—A report to the Criminology Research Advisory Council.* Australian Institute of Criminology. Retrieved October 24, 2024, from https://www.aic.gov.au/sites/default/files/2022-08/crg_0218_19_preventing_image-based.pdf

Flynn, A., Clough, J., & Cooke, T. (2022b). Disrupting and preventing deepfake abuse: Exploring criminal law responses to AI Facilitated Abuse. In A. Powell, A. Flynn, & L. Sugiura (Eds.), *The Palgrave handbook of gendered violence and technology* (pp. 583–602). Palgrave Macmillan.

Flynn, A., Scott, A. J., & Cama, E. (2024a). An empirical research study on barriers, facilitators, and strategies to promote bystander intervention in intimate image abuse contexts. In K. Summerer & G. M. Caletti (Eds.), *Criminalising intimate image abuse* (pp. 376–399). Oxford University Press.

Flynn, A., Powell, A., Scott, A. J., & Cama, E. (2022c). Deepfakes and digitally altered imagery abuse: A cross-country exploration of an emerging form of image-based sexual abuse. *British Journal of Criminology, 62*(6), 1341–1358. https://doi.org/10.1093/bjc/azab111

Flynn, A., & Henry, N. (2021). Image-based sexual abuse: An Australian reflection. *Women and Criminal Justice, 31*(4), 313–326. https://doi.org/10. 1080/08974454.2019.1646190

Flynn, A., Wheildon, L., Robards, B., Vakhitova, Z., & Harris, B. (2024b) *Australian users' experiences with control features on social media services and online dating apps: Key findings.* Retrieved October 21, 2024, from https:// research.monash.edu/files/571453440/australian_users_experiences_with_ control_features_on_social_media_services_and_online_dating_apps_final_r eport_may2023.pdf

Gilliam, M., Jagoda, P., Jaworski, E., Heberrt, L. E., Lyman, P., & Wilson, M. C. (2016). 'Because if we don't talk about it, how are we going to prevent it?': Lucidity, a narrative-based digital game about sexual violence. *Sex Education, 16*(4), 391–404. https://doi.org/10.1080/14681811.2015.1123147

Grant, J. M., Mottet, L. A., Tanis, J., Harrison, J., Herman, J. L., & Keisling, M. (2011). *Injustice at every turn: A report of the National Transgender Discrimination Survey.* Retrieved October 21, 2024, from https://transequality.org/ sites/default/files/docs/resources/NTDS_Report.pdf

Hamby, S. L., Weber, M. C., Grych, J. H., & Banyard, V. (2016). What difference do bystanders make? The association of bystander involvement with victim outcomes in a community sample. *Psychology of Violence, 6*(1), 91–102. https://doi.org/10.1037/a0039073

Henry, N., Flynn, A., & Powell, A. (2019). *Responding to revenge pornography: The scope, nature and impact of Australian criminal laws—A report to the Criminology Research Council.* Australian Institute of Criminology. Retrieved October 21, 2024, from https://www.aic.gov.au/sites/default/files/2020- 05/CRG_08_15-16-FinalReport.pdf

Hudson, H., Fetro, J., & Ogletree, R. (2014). Behavioral indicators and behaviors related to sexting among undergraduate students. *American Journal of Health Education, 45*(3), 183–195. https://doi.org/10.1080/19325037. 2014.901113

Israel, T., Harkness, A., Delucio, K., Ledbetter, J. N., & Avellar, T. R. (2013). Evaluation of police training on LGBTQ issues: Knowledge, interpersonal apprehension, and self-efficacy. *Journal of Police and Criminal Psychology, 29*(2), 1–11. https://doi.org/10.1007/s11896-013-9132-z

Kaya, A., Le, T. P., Brady, J., & Iwamoto, D. (2019). Men who intervene to prevent sexual assault: A grounded theory study on the role of masculinity in bystander intervention. *Psychology of Men & Masculinities, 21*(3), 463–478. https://doi.org/10.1037/men0000249

Kroshus, E. (2018). College athletes, pluralistic ignorance and bystander behaviors to prevent sexual assault. *Journal of Clinical Sport Psychology, 13*(2), 330–344. https://doi.org/10.1123/jcsp.2018-0039

Langenderfer-Magruder, L., Whitfield, D. L., Walls, N. E., Kattari, S. K., & Ramos, D. (2016). Experiences of intimate partner violence and subsequent police reporting among lesbian, gay, bisexual, transgender, and queer adults in Colorado: Comparing rates of cisgender and transgender victimization. *Journal of Interpersonal Violence, 31*(5), 855–871. https://doi.org/10.1177/0886260514556767

Lodge, J., & Frydenberg, E. (2005). The role of peer bystanders in school bullying: Positive steps toward promoting peaceful schools. *Theory into Practice, 44*(4), 329–336.

Miles-Johnson, T. (2016). Policing diversity: Examining police resistance to training reforms for transgender people in Australia. *Journal of Homosexuality, 63*(1), 103–106. https://doi.org/10.1080/00918369.2015.1078627

Office of the eSafety Commissioner. (2017). *Image-based abuse: National survey—Summary report*. Retrieved 21 October, 2024, from https://www.esafety.gov.au/about-us/research/image-based-abuse

Paradiso, M. N., Rollè, L., & Trombetta, T. (2024). Image-based sexual abuse associated factors: A systematic review. *Journal of Family Violence, 39*, 931–954. https://doi.org/10.1007/s10896-023-00557-z

Pina, A., Holland, J., & James, M. (2017). The malevolent side of revenge porn proclivity: Dark personality traits and sexist ideology. *International Journal of Technoethics, 8*(1), 30–43. https://doi.org/10.4018/IJT.2017010103

Powell, A., Scott, A. J., Flynn, A., & Henry, N. (2020). *Image-based sexual abuse: An international study of victims and perpetrators*. RMIT University. Retrieved October 21, 2024, from https://www.researchgate.net/public ation/339488012_Image-based_sexual_abuse_An_international_study_of_v ictims_and_perpetrators

Schewe, P. A. (2007). Interventions to prevent sexual violence. In L. Doll, E. N. Haas, S. Bonzo, D. Sleet, & J. Mercy (Eds.), *Handbook of injury and violence prevention* (pp. 223–240). Springer Science & Business Media.

Scott, A. J., & Gavin, J. (2018). Revenge pornography: The influence of perpetrator-victim sex, observer sex and observer sexting experience on perceptions of seriousness and responsibility. *Journal of Criminal Psychology, 8*(2), 162–172. https://doi.org/10.1108/JCP-05-2017-0024

Silver, E., & Miller, L. L. (2004). Sources of informal social control in Chicago neighborhoods. *Criminology, 42*(3), 551–583. https://doi.org/10.1111/j.1745-9125.2004.tb00529.x

Voelpel, S. C., Eckhoff, R. A., & Forster, J. (2008). David against Goliath? Group size and bystander effects in virtual knowledge sharing. *Human Relations, 61*(2), 271–295. https://doi.org/10.1177/0018726707087787

Van Ouytsel, J., Punyanunt-Carter, N. M., Walrave, M., & Ponnet, K. (2020a). Sexting within young adults' dating and romantic relationships. *Current Opinion in Psychology, 36*, 55–59. https://doi.org/10.1016/j.copsyc.2020.04.007

Van Ouytsel, J., Walrave, M., De Marez, L., Vanhaelewyn, B., & Ponnet, K. (2020b). Sexting, pressured sexting and image-based sexual abuse among a weighted-sample of heterosexual and LGB-youth. *Computers in Human Behavior, 117*. https://doi.org/10.1016/j.chb.2020.106630

Wamboldt, A., Khan, S. R., Mellins, C. A., & Hirsch, J. S. (2019). Friends, strangers, and bystanders: Informal practices of sexual assault intervention. *Global Public Health, 14*(1), 53–64. https://doi.org/10.1080/17441692.2018.1472290

Zvi, L., & Bitton, M. S. (2020). Perceptions of victim and offender culpability in non-consensual distribution of intimate images. *Psychology, Crime & Law, 27*(5), 427–442. https://doi.org/10.1080/1068316X.2020.1818236

Appendix

Table A.1 Two versions of the focus group scenarios

Scenario 1 (S1)
Maryam (woman, aged 21) has been seeing your friend Kai (man, aged 25) for about a week. Without any prior discussion, Maryam sends Kai a photo of herself completely naked. The next day, Kai shows the photo to a group of his friends (including you) during a broad discussion about sex.
In the alternate version, Maryam (victim-survivor) was replaced with Arjun (man, aged 25) and Kai (perpetrator) was replaced with Sarah (woman, aged 21).

Scenario 2 (S2)
You are on a train sitting near a transwoman named Alex (who you don't know). She is wearing a t-shirt and a skirt and is 20 years old. A 30-year-old man named Lou (who you also don't know) is sitting opposite Alex. He tries to engage Alex in conversation, but it is clear she doesn't know him, so she ignores him. Later, you see Lou using his iPhone to secretly take a photo up Alex's skirt. Alex doesn't know Lou has done this.
In the alternate scenario, Lou's (perpetrator) gender is changed to a woman.

The manufacturer's authorised representative in the EU is Springer
Nature Customer Service Centre GmbH, Europaplatz 3, 69115 Heidelberg,
Germany. If you have any concerns regarding our products, please
contact ProductSafety@springernature.com

Printed and bound by CPI Group (UK) Ltd, Croydon, CR0 4YY
27/04/2026
02097563-0017